HYPERACTIVITY
WHY WON'T MY CHILD PAY ATTENTION?

Sam Goldstein, PhD
Michael Goldstein, MD

John Wiley & Sons, Inc.
New York • Chichester • Brisbane • Toronto • Singapore

This text is printed on acid-free paper.

This publication is designed to provide accurate and
authoritative information in regard to the subject
matter covered. It is sold with the understanding that
the publisher is not engaged in rendering legal, accounting,
or other professional service. If legal advice or other
expert assistance is required, the services of a competent
professional person should be sought. *From a Declaration
of Principles jointly adopted by a Committee of the
American Bar Association and a Committee of Publishers.*

Library of Congress Cataloging-in-Publication Data

Goldstein, Sam
    Hyperactivity : why won't my child pay attention? / Sam Goldstein,
Michael Goldstein.
       p.   cm.
    "A common sense approach to understanding, negotiating the medical
and non-medical maze of evaluation and treatment, and successfully
managing the problems of children with attention-deficit
hyperactivity disorder."
    Includes bibliographical references.
    ISBN 0-471-53077-8 (cloth)   ISBN 0-471-53307-6 (paper)
    1. Attention-deficit hyperactivity disorder—Popular works.
2. Hyperactive children. I. Goldstein, Michael, 1945–
II. Title.
RJ606.H9G65   1992
61892'8589—dc20   91-24325
                                    CIP

Printed in the United States of America

10 9 8 7 6

Foreword

For the past several decades, the study of attention deficit disorder (ADD or ADHD) has captured the interest of medical, psychological, and educational researchers. The scientific investigation into the disorder has focused on a myriad of aspects including: epidemiology, etiology, methods of diagnosis, and procedures for treatment. It is likely that no other psychomedical disorder of childhood has been so well studied as ADD. One of the reasons for such intense interest is that ADD is fairly prevalent in our society, affecting 3 to 5 percent of the nation's school-age children. For many of these children, the effects of ADD will be noticeable throughout much of their youth and possibly into their adult years. Its effect on quality of life is dramatic, not only for the ADD child, but for his or her entire family as well.

Outcome studies indicate that ADD children are most likely to develop social, emotional, and behavioral disorders and will manifest more academic problems than non-ADD children. Many receive treatment for their disorder from pediatricians, mental health professionals, or educators. Those who are bright, non-aggressive, and come from stable and emotionally healthy families will fare better than those who are combative, learning impaired, or do not have the consistency of a stable family to rely on for guidance and support.

Despite the significant impact that ADD has on our children, for a great while there was little accurate information on the subject available to the public. Parents of children with ADD had to rely primarily on books written for other similar conditions such as learning disability or emotional disturbance for help. This stemmed, in part, from the early notions that ADD was not, in and of itself, a distinct disorder, but merely a subtype of other childhood learning or emotional problems. In the last several years, parents of ADD children began to seek more information to explain their children's unique and special difficulties. Fueled by a highly emotional mixture of love, confusion, hope, and desperation the ADD parent movement began. It took off like a shooting star and information about ADD began to pour in. This information became readily available to parents through community support groups, public libraries, or local book sellers.

Drs. Sam and Michael Goldstein have made much of this information available through their writings, video presentations, and public speaking across the country. Their latest book, *Hyperactivity: Why Won't My Child Pay Attention?*, is an excellent resource for parents who want to know about the basics of ADD and a lot more. This family guide is truly what its title implies, practical information presented in a straightforward manner to assist parents in understanding why their child won't pay attention. The authors guide parents through the process of diagnosis and explain the many aspects of treatment typically used to help ADD children. Sections on medication management, behavior modification, social skills training, communication building, and education are clearly presented. Suggestions for helping the ADD child through the adolescent period gives parents of younger children a glimpse into the future and those with adolescents an opportunity to see their teenager's behavior in a different light. A section on adult ADD offers all parents a glimpse into what may be their child's future struggle and promise.

The ADD movement is growing quickly and it will continue to have a dramatically positive effect on how children, adolescents, and adults with ADD are treated. With continued understanding through education the future of ADD children will become much more enlightened than was their past. Thanks to Dr. Sam Goldstein and Dr. Michael Goldstein for their continuing efforts to shed light on the needs of ADD children and their families. They certainly continue to guide us in the right directions.

HARVEY C. PARKER, PhD

Executive Director, Co-Founder
CH.A.D.D. (Children with Attention
Deficit Disorder)
August 1991

Preface

This book is about children who have difficulty paying attention, controlling emotions, and governing physical activity, and who do not think before they act. It is a book about children who are often described as taking unnecessary risks, but it begins with the premise that these children can succeed at home, in school, and in the community. They can manage these difficulties. Most importantly, when they become successful adults, they can make a significant positive contribution to society. Our obligation as parents and professionals is to understand these children and find ways to help them succeed.

This book also begins with the idea that problems that cannot be cured must be effectively managed, and effective management comes about through understanding those problems. To help your hyperactive child succeed, it is essential to understand your child's behavior, see the world through your child's eyes, and make the distinction between behavior that results from lack of ability and behavior that results from deliberate noncompliance.

Over the past hundred years, problems characteristic of hyperactive children have been categorized and labeled many different ways. At various times in the twentieth century, these children have been referred to as having the *fidgeties, a defect in moral control, minimal brain dysfunction, postencephalitic disorder, minimal brain damage, hyperkinesis, hyperkinetic reaction of childhood, attention deficit disorder, and attention-deficit hyperactivity disorder.* Although the label has changed repeatedly, the problem has not— it has remained fairly constant over time.

For the purposes of this book, problems of inattention, distractibility, restlessness, excessive activity, excessive emotionality, and impulsiveness will be referred to as problems of *childhood hyperactivity* or *hyperactivity.* The term hyperactivity is used because it is brief, simple, familiar, and in many clinical, research, and practical ways may best describe these children. Most are hyperactive in thought and action.

As professionals who deal with hyperactivity day in and day out, we spend a great deal of time educating parents and the general public about these problems. But this is only half the battle because we also must refute and challenge the myths of hyperactivity. Fully half the information the public has about hyperactivity may be erroneous. Misinformation ranges from gross distortions, (hyperactivity is caused by fluorescent lights) to misrepresentation (inattention can be cured through repetitive practice). For these reasons, a number of chapters at the outset of this book inform parents about the current scientific position and trends concerning the cause, course, evaluation, and prognosis of hyperactive children. Of course parents must also possess a realistic understanding of appropriate medical and nonmedical treatments. There is no sure cure or simple solution, and our critical review of these treatments offers practical guidelines to help you and your child.

Throughout this book, we have used the pronoun *he* when referring to the hyperactive child. This stylistic convention is for ease of reading only; the information herein refers impartially to girls and boys unless the specific content states otherwise.

The Appendix at the end of the book provides information for obtaining books, as well as other learning resources discussed in the text. It is crucial for parents to understand that no book can substitute for working with a well-informed professional. Most professionals agree, however, that the most critical variable for success for the hyperactive child is not any single treatment but patient, understanding, supportive parents who accept their child and are knowledgeable about hyperactivity. You will make an important difference. You can and must be those parents.

SAM GOLDSTEIN, PHD
MICHAEL GOLDSTEIN, MD

Neurology, Learning and Behavior Center
Salt Lake City, Utah
August 1992

Acknowledgments

This work is dedicated to our wives, Janet and Barbara, and our children, Allyson, Ryan, Rachel, Elizabeth, and Adam. Children are our best teachers. We have learned much from ours and yours. Once again we are indebted to Kathleen Gardner and Sarah Cheminant for their assistance in the preparation of this manuscript. Thanks also to Toni Kamins for her thoughtful editorial assistance.

This work is also dedicated to the memory of David Watson.

S.G.
M.G.

Trademarks

The following registered trademarks are used:

Catapres	Prozac
Cylert	Ritalin
Desoxyn	Ritalin S.R. 20
Dexedrine	Tegretol
Dilantin	Thorazine
Haldol	Tofranil
Nutrasweet	

Contents

About the Authors

SAM GOLDSTEIN, PhD, is a child psychologist and a director of the Neurology, Learning and Behavior Center in Salt Lake City. **MICHAEL GOLDSTEIN, MD,** is a child neurologist and a director of the Neurology, Learning and Behavior Center in Salt Lake City. They are known nationally for training parents and professionals to deal with problems of hyperactive children. Authors of several professional books on hyperactivity, including their very influential, professional bestseller, *Managing Attention Disorders in Children,* they are also the producers of the renowned video, *Why Won't My Child Pay Attention?,* which won several awards, including a Telly (the broadcast equivalent of an EMMY), and was a finalist in the New York Film Festival.

PART I

HYPERACTIVITY AND ITS CAUSES

CHAPTER 1

What Is Hyperactivity?

> George, a 9-year-old in the third grade, has boundless energy and frequently exercises poor judgment. His impulsive, inattentive behavior leads to his taking many risks and results in multiple problems at home and school. George's brothers and sisters are frequently unhappy with his behavior toward them, their possessions, and friends. His parents cannot cope with what seems to be resistance to responsible behavior. George's teachers are frustrated too by his inattentive, impulsive style, which often results in misbehavior and poor work habits. On the playground, although he has some friends, George is unable to follow the game rules and has poor problem-solving skills. He is frequently sought out by his peers when something dangerous needs doing such as climbing roofs or running across busy streets to retrieve balls, and he can be counted on to immerse himself in an activity.

The hyperactive child presents a significant challenge for parents and teachers. Researchers have suggested that hyperactivity may be the most common, persistent problem of childhood. It is persistent or chronic because there is no cure and the many problems facing hyperactive children must be managed day in and day out throughout childhood and adolescence. Problems resulting from hyperactivity may be among the most common reasons for referring childhood behavior problems to physicians, psychologists, educators, and other mental health specialists.

Inattention, restlessness, excessive activity, emotionality, impulsiveness, and difficulty delaying rewards affect children's interaction with their entire world: home, school, and the community at large. Relationships with parents, teachers, brothers, and sisters are frequently impaired because of the stress provoked by uneven, unpredictable behavior, and academic progress and personality development may be also negatively affected.

It is important to understand that the hyperactive child is exhibiting the most common childhood difficulties in a greatly exaggerated form. For most affected children, inattention, excessive activity or emotionally, and impulsive, nonthinking behavior result from temperament. This term describes a set of innate qualities children bring to the world with them. Many researchers believe that these qualities, which may be inherited, are the result of some specific imbalance in brain chemistry. Some children, however, may exhibit symptoms of hyperactivity as a result of anxiety, frustration, depression, or ineffective parenting. We are concerned here with the temperamentally hyperactive child. Later on, we will discuss the differences between these children and those with hyperactive symptoms that reflect other childhood problems.

By the time a teacher, friend, or physician suggests having your child evaluated for hyperactive behavior, in all likelihood, you have been coping with not one or two problems but a complex set of problems that affect your child in all areas of his or her environment. In addition, your child's problems can be exacerbated by social and nonsocial factors including health, diet, friends, learning problems, siblings, and even your own emotional state. For example, if you have had a difficult day at work, and are in a bad mood when you arrive home, you may overreact to a relatively minor problem. If, on top of this, your child is hyperactive, the combination may be a time bomb waiting to explode. Careful evaluation is necessary to determine the origin of the problem: you or your child.

Dr. Keith Conners, a well-known researcher in the field of childhood hyperactivity, has noted that evaluation for hyperactivity is complicated. There is no absolute, diagnostic test for hyperactivity.

It requires the careful collection of information from a variety of sources (i.e., parents and teachers), by a variety of means (i.e., questionnaires, interviews, and testing), in a variety of ways. In addition, there are no positive markers in a child's developmental history that will absolutely diagnose hyperactivity. Though certain early childhood developmental factors (i.e., the difficult-to-comfort infant or the infant with sleep difficulty) may place children at risk, hyperactivity is marked by a cluster of these problems, their intensity or severity, and their persistence as the child grows.

It is also important for parents to understand that hyperactivity is best described as an exaggeration of what may be age-appropriate behavior. A child may be too active or not attentive enough. Other problems of childhood are ordinarily defined in a black-and-white fashion. For example, a child may or may not be setting fires. There is no gray area. Hyperactivity, on the other hand, has a very large gray area in which the child's levels of attention, activity, and impulse are determined both by the child's temperament and by the demands placed on the child by the world. Hyperactivity must thus be considered an interaction disorder. The amount of trouble a restless child will experience is, in part, determined by the situation. On the playground, the restless child may experience little difficulty because he isn't being asked to sit still. In a restaurant, however, the child's restlessness becomes a problem.

It is also unfair to say that an inattentive child can never pay attention, an impulsive child can never plan an action, or a restless child can never sit still. Hyperactivity is best described as the cause of problems that result from inconsistency rather than inability. Hyperactivity results in inconsistent performance. This pattern creates frequent frustration. In one situation, the child can pay attention, yet he is distracted a few moments later. One minute the child may be sitting, listening to the teacher, yet a few moments later something very minor proves to be a distraction.

Hyperactivity is not limited to school-age children. Although professionals may not apply the label to a child until he or she is at least five, many younger children exhibit similar symptoms that can be early indicators of the problem. In addition, almost as many teenagers experience hyperactivity as do younger children. Although hyperactive adolescents may experience very different problems, they struggle nonetheless. In many ways, hyperactive adolescents experience more complex problems as they attempt to move into adulthood. Finally, some research studies indicate that as many as one third to one half of hyperactive children present with what becomes a lifelong set of problems. Factors affecting the adult life of hyperactive children will be discussed in a later chapter.

For the hyperactive child, daily life is a series of challenges brought about by a number of specific skill deficiencies or weaknesses. If we were to take 100 hyperactive children, as a group they would share similar weaknesses—difficulty paying attention, controlling their body and emotions, and thinking before acting. However, as we have explained, problems not only stem from skill weaknesses but result from the child's inability to meet the demands placed on him by the world. Thus, a hyperactive child living on a deserted tropical island may not develop significant problems from these temperamental qualities. Any 2 of these 100 hyperactive children may experience very different problems because they have different parents, teachers, siblings, and so on. Attempting to understand hyperactivity by focusing on specific problems rather than skill weaknesses may cloud rather than improve understanding.

A century ago in our educational system, a teacher's usual method of dealing with these temperamental difficulties was to hit the child soundly with a ruler. If the ruler broke before the child, authorities politely suggested the child not return to school. Thus, school difficulties were solved and the child was sent out into the world. In our society and culture, whether good or bad, right or wrong, we place a high premium on children sitting still, paying attention, and planning and arriving at finished products. These demands are made on even younger children. The hyperactive child, unable to meet these demands, is an immediate candidate for a myriad of problems.

A COMMON-SENSE DESCRIPTION
OF HYPERACTIVITY

The common-sense description of hyperactivity has four components:

1. *Inattention and Distractibility.* Hyperactive children have difficulty concentrating on tasks and paying attention consistently compared with their peers. The more boring, uninteresting or repetitive the task, the more difficulty encountered. Attention, however, is a complex process consisting of different skills. For example, to function effectively in the classroom, a child must master a number of attention-oriented skills. These include the ability to focus attention appropriately at any given moment, to begin an assigned task, to sustain attention long enough for task completion, to ignore distractions, to divide attention (i.e., be able to take notes and listen to the teacher at the same time), and to be vigilant or ready to respond during group activities.

2. *Overarousal and Excessive Activity.* Hyperactive children tend to be excessively restless, overactive, and easily provoked to excessive emotion. They have difficulty controlling their bodies in situations that require them to sit still for a long time. Their emotional reactions are more intense and more frequent than those of other children. This occurs regardless of the emotion being expressed—anger, frustration, happiness, or sadness. As one parent reported, his hyperactive child wears his emotions on his sleeve. The term *overarousal* appears to best describe these tendencies.

3. *Impulsiveness.* Hyperactive children have difficulty thinking before they act. As author and researcher Dr. Russell Barkley has described, they have difficulty following rules. They often understand and know the rules, but their need to act quickly overwhelms their limited ability for self-control. This results in inappropriate, nonthinking behavior.

Hyperactive children are frequently repeat offenders. Although this sounds like a criminal term, it is the best description of the inability to benefit from experience. These children require more supervision and frequently frustrate parents and teachers. Most children, after their third or fourth time of engaging in a restricted behavior, remember their caretaker's anger and punishments. The offending behavior usually stops. The hyperactive child, however, does not appear to benefit from that experience. You may tell such a child to stay out of something a dozen times, but he will still repeat the forbidden activity for the thirteenth time. Frequently, parents label this behavior purposeful, noncaring, or oppositional. It is quite likely, however, that this does not accurately describe it. The child's problems usually stem from incompetence, inconsistency, or inability rather than disobedience.

4. *Difficulty with Rewards.* Hyperactive children have difficulty working toward long-term goals. They require repeated short-term payoffs rather than a single long-term reward. Some researchers have suggested that rewards may be ineffective in changing the behavior of hyperactive children and have described this behavior as a motivational deficit. While biological or temperamental explanations for difficulty with rewards certainly make sense, there is also a learned component to this problem—what psychologists call negative reinforcement.

Negative reinforcement means you do something aversive to your child to change his behavior, whereas positive reinforcement means you reward the child for behavior you wish to strengthen. Frequently, the behavior of hyperactive children results in large amounts of negative reinforcement as parents attempt to control the child. For example, a father might use threats to get the child to come to the dinner table, or a mother might come into her son's room when he is supposed to be dressing and remind him to return to dressing when he is off task. When she walks out, however, he may stop dressing. As long as his mother bothers him, he continues dressing, but he would much rather be playing with his toys. In this situation, the mother is the negative reinforcer—she is his reason for returning to a task the child does not want to do. Thus hyperactive children begin to view the world as a place where you work to get rid of what you do not want (i.e., bugging from parents) rather than where you strive to earn things you desire.

Consider for a moment the negative impact on a child's life if he or she experiences the four skill weaknesses characteristic of hyperactivity. A child ineffective or incompetent in one, two, or four of these skills is significantly compromised in the ability to negotiate life successfully. Can children be weak in just one or two of these skills and not others? Absolutely. Hyperactive children, however, are usually weak in all four.

Further, the demands placed on children are primarily determined by the adults in their lives. Hyperactive adults can modify their lives to minimize negative experiences. Hyperactive children cannot. Also, weaknesses in these four skills and the resultant problems appear to have a significant impact on a child's personality and thought development.

As we have noted in *Managing Attention Disorders in Children*, our text for professionals, a hyperactive child who experiences years of negative feedback, negative reinforcement, and an inability to meet the reasonable demands of family, friends, and school could certainly be affected for life. Parents and professionals must be concerned not only with the skill deficits and immediate problems but also with the significant long-term problems.

HOW MANY CHILDREN ARE HYPERACTIVE?

In the 1950s when teachers were asked to identify hyperactive children in their classroom, some nominated half of their students. Other, more recent studies have suggested that as many as 20% to 25% of school-age children may experience problems of hyperactivity. How can this be? Is this childhood problem so common or could these high estimates be the result of insufficient information?

Over the past 10 years, the professional community has developed more efficient diagnostic techniques. Today, professionals ask a series of questions concerning hyperactivity and the problems these children experience. Accurate evaluation seeks to observe a consistency in problems in a variety of settings (i.e., home and school) and agreement between a number of raters, including parents, teachers, and community-based professionals. Since as children grow older they experience less trouble with some problems of hyperactivity, a thorough evaluation gathers a careful history and seeks to determine that a particular child's skills are significantly weaker than other children of the same sex and age.

When all the evaluation criteria are met, the presence of hyperactivity in childhood is approximately 3% to 5%. Higher percentages seem to occur in certain populations such as children from low-income families. Research has also consistently suggested that hyperactivity is approximately five to nine times more frequent in boys than girls, although some problems of hyperactivity may affect an equal number of boys and girls. For example, it has been suggested that girls experience problems completing classwork as often as boys. There is no doubt, however, that more boys experience inattention, restlessness, impulsiveness, and temper problems than girls.

Some studies have suggested that hyperactive girls may experience more problems with mood and emotion and fewer problems with aggression than hyperactive boys. Other researchers have found hyperactive girls display more conduct problems than hyperactive boys. Still, other studies have reported that hyperactive girls may experience greater learning and language problems. Although it may not be possible to draw firm conclusions about the differences between hyperactive boys and girls, it is fair to say that although the numbers favor boys, there are more similarities than differences in their behavior.

ARE ALL HYPERACTIVE CHILDREN OVERACTIVE?

Until 1980, hyperactivity was the term used by the professional community to describe the inattentive, overactive, and impulsive child. From 1980 through 1987, the American Psychiatric Association changed the diagnostic label from *Hyperkinetic Reaction of*

Childhood to *Attention Deficit Disorder*. During this period, a child could be considered impulsive and inattentive without being excessively overactive. In 1987, the diagnostic system was changed again, and the skill weaknesses of these children were officially labeled *Attention-deficit Hyperactivity Disorder*. At the same time a professional committee decided that the majority of children experiencing problems of inattention and impulsiveness also experienced problems of overactivity. This change was not well received by the professional community, and in all likelihood the clinical definition and/or the label will change again. A distinction will probably be made between children experiencing difficulty paying attention and those experiencing a wider range of skill deficits, including inattention, overactivity, and impulsiveness.

Are these differences between the inattentive, restless child and the inattentive, calm child? A large volume of literature suggests that this may be so. It may be the excessive activity level that results in frequent referrals to child guidance clinics and special education teams. In studies of hyperactive children referred to clinics three to five times more youngsters are overactive than are non-overactive. Other researchers, however, have suggested that inattention without overactivity may occur twice as frequently as inattention with overactivity in the nonreferred childhood population. The non-overactive, inattentive child may not be referred or may be described as anxious, withdrawn, poorly motivated, or learning disabled rather than hyperactive.

In comparison, the inattentive, hyperactive, and impulsive child appears to have more problems with aggression, is more unpopular, and has greater difficulty with conduct. The inattentive child who is not overactive or impulsive may be described as shy, socially isolated, moderately unpopular, and poor at sports. This child's difficulty with athletics may not necessarily result from a lack of ability, but from a tendency to not pay attention during organized sports. This child may be on the other side of the soccer field watching the clouds go by as the other children play the game. Approximately 20% to 30% of hyperactive children appear primarily to experience problems of inattention without significant problems of overactivity or impulsivity.

Research studies have consistently found that hyperactive children are more likely to develop depression or anxiety, exhibit disruptive behavior, and have poorer school performance, more learning disabilities, problems with friends, and weaker self-concept than do unaffected children of the same age.

REMEMBER . . .

✦ Hyperactivity results from four kinds of skill weakness (attention, impulse, arousal, and rewards or motivation) which may cause problems at home, school, and with friends.

✦ Problems occur based on the child's skill weaknesses and the demands placed on the child by the world.

✦ Most hyperactive children are inattentive, impulsive, overactive, and overemotional and have difficulty with motivation and delaying rewards. About 20% to 30% are primarily inattentive.

✦ Hyperactivity is best described as resulting from inconsistency or incompetence rather than misbehavior or noncompliance.

✦ The most likely cause of hyperactivity is inheritance.

✦ Parents do not cause hyperactivity but their behavior can determine the number of problems at home, school, or with friends.

✦ Hyperactivity affects more boys than girls.

✦ Boys and girls can experience equal problems as the result of hyperactivity.

✦ Hyperactivity cannot be cured and must be effectively managed throughout childhood.

✦ Approximately 3% to 5% of all children experience problems resulting from hyperactivity.

CHAPTER 2

Evaluating the Child for Hyperactivity

From the time she started school, Alice's teachers complained that she often appeared to be daydreaming, did not complete her work, and was extremely restless. By the third grade, these problems were of even greater concern. Despite excellent academic skills, Alice was not performing well in the classroom. She had a small network of friends and was not a behavior problem at home, and a visit to the family physician produced a clean bill of health. Alice did not appear to be hyperactive since she was able to sit still and pay attention during the physical examination. A neighbor suggested Alice's problems might result from vitamin deficiency and provided the family with an article from a popular magazine. For a few months the family tried this vitamin therapy, but with little success. Then a relative suggested that the problem might relate to Alice's diet. The family diligently attempted to change her diet as prescribed by a book purchased at the mall. Although Alice appeared somewhat better initially, it did not last. After a few months and considerable effort and expense, Alice's problems remained unchanged. Finally, the family watched a commercial on television suggesting that all children could succeed and that the secrets to success could be found in a video purchased for $89.95. Once again, the family invested time and money and again had little success. Finally, Alice's father concluded that there really was nothing wrong with his daughter. This was just how she was going to be and there was no need to seek further professional or popular treatment.

When we ask parents of hyperactive children how they first knew there was something different about their child, we receive varied answers. Some parents report an awareness of the child's differences almost from birth. One mother recalled her child's high pitched, frequent screams. Another reported difficulty comforting her child. One father recalled his child's boundless energy and poor judgment beginning as soon as the child was able to walk. Still another parent recalled observing the differences between her child and the others the first time her child entered preschool.

Unfortunately, no single, or fixed set of factors signal the possibility of hyperactivity. Although many behavioral and developmental factors suggest hyperactivity, other childhood problems could cause these very same factors. In addition the large body of misinformation further complicates parents' ability to recognize a problem and subsequently negotiate the medical and mental health maze.

Alice's parents are not unique in their experiences. The intervention parents attempt and the information they receive concerning hyperactivity from people they perceive as knowledgeable various greatly. How then should parents proceed? We suggest that parents first separate behavior from cause and diagnosis. It is your job to be able to recognize characteristics in your child which distress and concern you. The set of checklists in this chapter may help you. We also provide guidelines that, as Dr. Michael Gordon has written, will help you "seek the best in evaluation before you seek the best in treatment."

IS YOUR CHILD AT RISK FOR HYPERACTIVITY?

This set of questionnaires will help you organize your thoughts about hyperactive behaviors. Remember, questionnaires do not diagnose or explain cause. Questionnaires simply describe behavior. For these questionnaires, no scores are generated based on your answers and they are not compared with any sample population.

If your child is having problems and the majority of your answers on the applicable questionnaires are yes, you have sufficient reason to seek professional assistance to determine if your child is hyperactive. On the other hand, you do not have sufficient reason to believe your child *is* hyperactive. A diagnosis must be made by one or more trained professionals familiar with childhood behavior. These professionals must be willing to spend the necessary time to evaluate your child. As we will explain, the diagnosis of hyperactivity cannot be made based on a single problem, questionnaire, or brief checkup.

Take a few minutes and fill out the applicable questionnaires.

PRESCHOOL AND TODDLER QUESTIONNAIRE FOR PARENT

Compared with other children, my child:

	Yes	No
Seems as if he is driven by a motor.	———	———
Is constantly on the go.	———	———
Has trouble staying in one place for even short periods of time.	———	———
Pays attention only to very stimulating events and then for only short periods of time.	———	———
Doesn't adapt well to change.	———	———
Becomes overemotional easily.	———	———
Cries frequently and with great intensity.	———	———
Is usually unpredictable in behavior and routines such as sleep and meals.	———	———
Seems more excitable than other children.	———	———
Often acts without thinking.	———	———
Leaves even simple tasks unfinished.	———	———
Usually pays attention for only a few minutes at a time.	———	———
Becomes frustrated easily.	———	———

SCHOOL-AGE CHILD QUESTIONNAIRE FOR PARENT

Compared with other children, my child:

	Yes	No
Seems more excitable.	____	____
Often acts without thinking.	____	____
Cries easily and often.	____	____
Has difficulty controlling emotions.	____	____
Can't seem to sit still in the car, restaurants, church, etc.	____	____
Fidgets when seated.	____	____
Leaves many tasks unfinished.	____	____
Usually pays attention for only short periods of time.	____	____
Pays attention if sufficiently motivated, such as playing a video game.	____	____
Becomes frustrated easily.	____	____
Acts too young.	____	____
Is overactive.	____	____
Daydreams.	____	____
Can't follow more than one or two instructions at a time.	____	____
Is disorganized.	____	____
Loses things necessary to complete tasks (i.e., homework).	____	____

ADOLESCENT QUESTIONNAIRE FOR PARENT

Compared with other teenagers, my adolescent:

	Yes	No
Has a history of poor school performance.	———	———
Has a history of frequent comments from past teachers concerning the need for better attention to task.	———	———
Often leaves tasks unfinished.	———	———
Was restless and overactive as a child.	———	———
Often acts without thinking.	———	———
Appears difficult to motivate.	———	———
Frustrates quickly.	———	———
Leaves many tasks unfinished.	———	———
Expresses a desire to succeed but then doesn't.	———	———
Seems very disorganized.	———	———
Daydreams.	———	———
Has trouble paying attention to routine activities.	———	———
Is disorganized.	———	———

QUESTIONNAIRE FOR TEACHERS

Compared with other children in the class my child:

	Yes	No
Completes less work.	_____	_____
Cannot work independently without the need for assistance.	_____	_____
Seems unable to follow simple directions accurately.	_____	_____
Seems unable to follow a sequence of directions accurately.	_____	_____
Frequently fidgets and gets up and out of seat.	_____	_____
Seems unable to efficiently control emotions.	_____	_____
Acts without thinking.	_____	_____
Talks too much.	_____	_____
Seems to daydream.	_____	_____
Requires more teacher time for academic, social, or emotional problems.	_____	_____
Seems disorganized.	_____	_____
Seems to have the ability to succeed but doesn't.	_____	_____
Seems inattentive.	_____	_____
Seems easily distracted.	_____	_____

ARMED WITH YOUR SUSPICIONS, NOW WHAT?

Some parents first learn that their child's temperament is creating problems from a teacher. Such children may be inattentive and disorganized, but not really hyperactive. In these situations, it is important for parents to understand their rights and obtain as much evaluation help as possible from school personnel. When the teacher complains of hyperactivity or inattention, request a meeting with the school psychologist. It is your right to ask the school psychologist to observe your child in the classroom, interview the child and teacher, and if possible, administer academic and psychological tests. You should expect the psychologist to describe your child's classroom problems and to define specifically what, why, when, and how problems occur. It is also fair to expect an explanation about the interventions that have been attempted. The checklist on page 20 shows the interventions teachers most frequently attempt in the classroom. Find out how many have been attempted for your child. Remember, according to U.S. and Canadian law, every child is entitled to a free appropriate education, and it must meet their academic, emotional, and social needs.

If the school team members (psychologist, special education teacher, principal, and classroom teacher) suspect your child is hyperactive, they will usually suggest you consult your family physician. Some teams blatantly suggest this because they want medication administered. Others are more conservative and suggest that these problems might be caused by other medical disorders. If the school team suggests that medication is the solution to your child's problems, remind them that pills will not substitute for skills. While medication may help hyperactive children with some skills, a variety of school-related problems must be dealt with through effective management and skill building. Both interventions will be explained later. Nevertheless, a consultation with the family physician is an essential part of the evaluation for hyperactivity. The physician's role includes directing the search for a specific medical cause participating in the diagnostic evaluation, and when medication is indicated, supervising a medication intervention program. Medical evaluation includes:

CHECKLIST OF CLASSROOM INTERVENTIONS USED

Child's Name _____

Teacher Name _____ Daytime Phone _____

School _____ Grade _____

Child's Primary Problems: _____

_____

_____

Please check any of the interventions listed below that you have attempted for my child. Your comments concerning the result of each intervention would also be helpful.

_____ Contracts   _____

_____ Parent Conference   _____

_____ Home Note   _____

_____ Monitor with Timing Device   _____

_____ Increased Supervision   _____

_____ Counseling   _____

_____ Response Cost Reinforcement   _____

_____ Peer Involvement   _____

_____ Tutoring   _____

_____ Direct Instruction   _____

_____ Use of Special Equipment
      (i.e., tape recorder)   _____

_____ In-school Suspension   _____

_____ Change in Classroom Environment
      (i.e., seating arrangement)   _____

_____ Change in Curriculum   _____

_____ Schedule Change   _____

_____ Teaching and Practicing of
      Expected Behavior with Student   _____

1. Searching for specific causes of hyperactivity that can be medically treated: hyperthyroidism, pinworms, sleep apnea, iron deficiency anemia, or side effects of other medications such as phenobarbital or anti-allergy drugs. Successful treatment of these conditions may lead to a reduction in hyperactive symptoms. The majority of hyperactive children, however, *do not* experience these problems. It is much more likely that their hyperactivity is related to a problem that cannot be medically cured such as certain birth factors, brain injury, and most commonly, heredity.

2. The physician must make a decision concerning the need for further medical diagnostic testing. Medical testing ranges from a simple blood count to a complex brain scan. Each test can rule out illnesses that can occasionally masquerade as hyperactivity. But these tests do not help make or confirm the diagnosis of hyperactivity, and unless there are specific indications of other medical disorders, such as a teacher's suspicion of seizures, these tests are usually not needed.

3. The physician must complete an appropriate physical and neurological examination. Research has suggested that medical factors, such as a child's ability to control motor movements, may provide valuable information indicating a physical basis for the cluster of hyperactivity symptoms. These findings, however, are less helpful than other tests for the diagnosis or exclusion of hyperactivity. Some of these findings are often present in normal children and may in fact be absent in children with hyperactivity. But this examination is important to help the physician identify the biological basis for the child's hyperactivity.

4. The physician must evaluate the risks and potential benefits of medication. Although the decision to use medication is part of the treatment process not the diagnostic process evaluating the risks versus benefits must be done at the outset. It is not appropriate for the physician to administer medication merely on suspicion of hyperactivity and then conclude hyperactivity if the child's symptoms improve. A family medical and social history may contain clues to mental illness or motor disorders, previous experience with hyperactivity medication or reactions to other

treatment programs. In addition, the child's medical history may reveal symptoms such as reactions to other medications, mental illness or growth or cardiovascular problems. This could suggest increased risk on medication. Medical evaluation is part of a multidisciplinary evaluation for hyperactivity. The physician alone, without the necessary supporting data concerning the child's history, behavior, emotional status, and school achievement cannot accurately make a diagnosis.

Finding a case manager can be difficult. Many family physicians consult a variety of medical and nonmedical individuals. Your physician probably consults a psychologist or psychiatrist about hyperactivity and related problems. We suggest that an expert evaluate every child suspected of being hyperactive. This person must provide a thorough description of the child's symptoms and demonstrate an understanding of the problems and the possible causes. The possibility that the child may be experiencing other mental health difficulties must be considered. Friends and neighbors may prove helpful by suggesting someone with whom they have worked successfully. Finally, some of the best referrals come from parent's support groups.

Many children suspected of being hyperactive require the expertise of a child psychiatrist because they may be experiencing coexisting severe problems such as depression, anxiety, destructive conduct, autism, or Tourette's syndrome. In such situations, a psychiatrist's perspective and experience with various treatments can be helpful.

INFORMATION NECESSARY FOR A
THOROUGH EVALUATION

A thorough evaluation of hyperactivity in childhood must include the collection and observation of eight kinds of information.

1. *History.* Be prepared to provide a thorough family and developmental history of your child. Historical information concerning other problems the family has experienced, methods used in

discipline, early signs of temperamental difficulty, and parents' memory of events in the child's life are critical to diagnosis. This is even more important in adolescents. A history suggesting long-standing problems of inattention, impulsiveness, and overactive behavior is the best single source of diagnostic information.

2. *Intelligence.* Difficult temperament has very little to do with intelligence. However, if you are going to act quickly and without thinking, the more intelligent you are, the more likely it is that you will be successful. If you are very bright in school, you may arrive at the correct answer without much effort. Intelligent children are also more likely to benefit from cognitive interventions and can develop insight about the impact their behavior has on others. Less intelligent children are less likely to be able to do this.

Children functioning well below average are much more likely to be frustrated by the increasingly complex demands of school and life. Therefore, they are more likely to exhibit hyperactivity problems as the result of frustration and not necessarily temperamental difficulty. Many tests are used by professionals purport to measure intelligence. But such measurement techniques tend to be subjective because there are many different theories about the definition of intelligence. It can be best thought of as an artificial idea that has been created by behavioral scientists. Intelligence is thought to be a set of skills and abilities that predict how well an individual may function in a variety of situations. So the term intelligence may mean something different to each of us. Do not be fooled by intelligence tests that simply ask a number of general questions or have the child draw a picture of a person. The best intelligence measures usually take at least one hour to complete and provide a broad overview of a child's verbal and nonverbal skills.

3. *Personality and Emotional Functioning.* Some hyperactive children are very aware of their problems and, as a result, become increasingly unhappy, helpless, and frustrated as they continue to fail. Others seem oblivious to their failure and happily proceed with their lives regardless of the number of frustrating events they experience. A thorough assessment of hyperactivity must include an evaluation of personality and current emotional functioning.

Evaluators must develop some understanding of children's level of confidence; how well children believe they are meeting expectations in their lives; how they feel about themselves and the people in their lives; and how aware they are of the difficulties they are experiencing. Such an assessment is often completed using a number of standardized questionnaires designed to evaluate depression, anxiety, and personality. Children complete these questionnaires and their answers are compared with a sample of normal children. This assessment usually includes an interview with the child.

4. *Academic Assessment.* By the high school years, the majority of hyperactive children are behind in at least one basic academic subject. So, thorough assessment of the child or adolescent's academic skills is an essential part of the evaluation. If the child is achieving at or above grade level, then a lack of performance in the classroom is less an immediate concern than if the child is behind and inattentive. In the latter case, direct intervention to improve academic skills as well as increase performance are needed. Remember that approximately 20% to 30% of hyperactive children also experience some specific skill weakness that interfere with their ability to learn. Treatments for hyperactivity, in all likelihood, will not have much effect on what these children are learning. They require direct, special instruction for their learning disability.

5. *Friends.* Remember that a child's ability to make and keep friends has been found to be an important, insulating factor in determining how well that child will fare behaviorally and emotionally during the course of childhood. An assessment of the child's friends and social skills is usually obtained through parent and teacher interviews, questionnaires, and an interview with the child.

6. *Discipline and Home Behavior.* The hyperactive child's behavior does not occur in isolation. The way parents interact with the child may not cause hyperactivity but is definitely a factor in determining how great or minimal the hyperactive child's problems at home may be. Be prepared to provide the evaluator with an explanation of your views on discipline and the types of discipline you have attempted.

7. *Classroom Behavior.* In addition to obtaining information about your child's school progress, a thorough evaluation must also include the teacher's perceptions and observations about your child's ability to follow rules and limits, and respect authority in the classroom. This information is often very helpful in understanding the manner in which the child is coping with hyperactive problems. When hyperactivity is not effectively managed in the classroom, some children withdraw and become even more inattentive. Others become oppositional, defiant, or class clowns.

8. *Medical.* As we have discussed, a medical evaluation is an essential part of the evaluation process.

A FIVE-STEP PROCESS TO DIAGNOSING HYPERACTIVITY

It is important for parents to understand that there is no single score or observation that either confirms or rules out the presence of hyperactivity in a child. Many attention, activity, and impulse problems, which are attributed to hyperactivity in some children, are also associated with other emotional and adjustment problems. It is important for the evaluator to carefully review a range of information before making the diagnosis. The eight types of information reviewed are organized into this five-step process. This helps avoid a false positive diagnosis, calling a child hyperactive when he is not, and a false negative diagnosis, calling a child something else when hyperactivity is the source of the problems.

The process by which your child is evaluated for hyperactivity should include five important steps. The first step is that your child's behavior must meet the definition of Attention-deficit Hyperactivity Disorder (ADHD) as described in the most current edition of the *Diagnostic and Statistical Manual of the American Psychiatric Association* (Washington, DC, 1987). Your child's hyperactive problems must have begun before age seven, not be the result of an autistic disorder, and have lasted longer than six months. According to the descriptors in this manual, a child must manifest a number of behaviors such as restless fidgeting, problems remaining seated, easy distraction, problems taking turns, impulsive responding, problems completing things, difficulty remaining on task, leaving many things unfinished, difficulty playing quietly, talking excessively, interrupting frequently, often not listening, being disorganized, and taking high risks.

Some medical and mental health practitioners make the diagnosis of hyperactivity based only on Step 1. This is dangerous. The American Psychiatric Association advocates that the diagnosis of Attention-deficit Hyperactivity Disorder should not be made solely on this definition. Additional information must be gathered. It is also difficult to use this definition accurately since a description of what is age appropriate is not provided, and this definition of ADHD sounds very much like most three-year-olds. They are not all hyperactive! Utilizing this definition alone also increases the risk of overdiagnosing hyperactivity in young children and underdiagnosing it in teenagers. Some researchers have suggested that if this step alone is used, as many as 25% of all school-age children could be identified as hyperactive. While this 25% probably includes all the children who are hyperactive, it also includes a much larger group who are not.

Step 2 involves use of well-developed parent and teacher questionnaires. These questionnaires have been proven accurate in identifying children who experience problems and skill weaknesses consistent with hyperactivity. Remember, however, that questionnaires do not diagnose, they only describe behavior. Beware of medical or mental health experts who base their diagnosis solely on the scores obtained from questionnaires.

Step 3 involves the collection of objective or scientific information concerning the child's behavior and skill weaknesses. It includes observation of the child's behavior in the classroom and direct testing of the child. The test's attempt to evaluate the child's ability to pay attention, plan, and organize through a variety of ways including paper-and-pencil tasks such as mazes. A child's ability to imitate motor movements successfully may also be sensitive. One of the most promising areas in assessment of hyperactive children is the use of computers. A number of programs have been designed to measure various attentional skills. These are slowly making their way into clinical practice. But at this time, the most widely used instrument is the Gordon Diagnostic System. This portable instrument contains a microprocessor capable of running a number of tasks that have proven to be very sensitive to identifying the impulsive, inattentive qualities of hyperactive children. It is gaining greater acceptance and is quickly becoming a standard in the field for objective assessment of hyperactivity. (For more information about the Gordon Diagnostic System, you can write to Gordon Systems, Inc., P.O. Box 746, DeWitt, New York 13214.)

Step 4 involves the careful evaluation of the child in a variety of settings. At the very least, these include home, school, and neighborhood. Remember, while hyperactive children do not experience the same severity of problems in all situations, they usually experience some difficulty in most daily situations. When problems occur specifically in one isolated setting, such as school or home, there is a greater likelihood that the hyperactive symptoms indicate some other difficulty.

The fifth and most important step is a careful consideration as to whether or not symptoms reflect some other emotional, learning, or medical disorder. For example, recently we evaluated a third grader. A review of situational problems indicated that this child only experienced problems in school. There was no longstanding history of hyperactive symptoms. These problems had evolved slowly over the past year. Further assessment revealed that this child was quite intelligent but was experiencing a specific memory disorder. Up through third grade, the youngster had been able to use his intellectual skills to compensate for memory problems, but he was unable to do so as the demands of school increased. As the result of frustration, symptoms of restlessness, apparent inattention, and impulsiveness developed.

It has been our experience that if a child fits into all five guidelines in this diagnostic process, there is a strong likelihood that the child's problems reflect a biological, temperamental disorder. It is also important for parents to remember that many hyperactive children experience other behavioral, emotional, or learning problems.

For children in whom symptoms appear to begin in kindergarten and increase as the child progresses through school, a careful review of learning skills and abilities is essential. The majority of children with a history of hyperactivity exhibit problems before entering school. Parents must not forget that hyperactive like problems frequently characterize children with language, social, learning, and behavioral difficulties.

WHAT TO EXPECT WHEN THE
EVALUATION IS OVER

When seeking an evaluation of their child, parents are consumers purchasing knowledge, information, and opinion. They are entitled to more than just a label or a five-minute explanation concerning the nature of the problem and its solution. At our Center, once an evaluation has been completed, the parents and evaluator, usually without the child or adolescent present, spend an hour reviewing all the gathered information. The evaluator tries to help parents see the world through the eyes of the child and to understand the process by which the evaluator arrived at the conclusions. It has been our experience that often when treatment fails, it is not because of inadequate evaluation and diagnosis, but because insufficient time was spent helping parents understand, from a practical and common-sense standpoint, their child's problems and the relationship of the treatment options to the diagnostic issues.

We also believe that parents are entitled to a written report. And whether it is 1 page or 10, it must summarize the evaluation process, the conclusions, the reasons for those conclusions, and treatment suggestions. At our Center, during a discussion of the evaluation, the evaluator tries to place the child in a real-life setting. Helping parents see the world through their child's eyes and understand the reasons and causes for the child's difficulties, helps the treatment process begin. It allows parents to play an active role and helps them make appropriate treatment decisions for their child. The following explanation was made to Alan's parents following his evaluation:

The information we collected reveals that Alan is very intelligent; when he first began school, he was able to use his intelligence to succeed. Although his teachers complained that he did not sit still or pay attention very well, they also reported that when he paid attention, his contribution and work completion were good. Alan began having problems in first and second grade and has difficulty being ready to respond and waiting while the teacher is speaking. He also has trouble deciding what to pay attention to and then settling down to work once he has decided to do so. In addition, he does not follow things through to completion. We have also discovered that Alan has problems controlling a pencil. Even when he pays attention, knows what to do, and gets started, it is difficult for him to place his work on the paper neatly and efficiently. During a spelling test, for example, even when he pays attention to the teacher and knows how to spell the word, it takes him longer ,than the other children to write down the word. By that time, the teacher may have moved on to another word, or Alan may become frustrated and not finish spelling the word correctly. He also appears somewhat impulsive and in situations where choices must be made, he tends to choose the path that involves the least effort and seems initially most attractive. He does not stop and use his intelligence to consider each choice carefully and make the best choice.

In the social realm, Alan's inability to plan, and his difficulty complimenting others and making appropriate requests results in other children not wanting to play with him. A pattern of negative reinforcement, both at home and at school, has resulted in Alan starting but never finishing difficult tasks. Alan is also aware of his problems and comments that he is not as smart as others nor does he behave as well as his brothers or sisters at home. The primary source of Alan's problem is his difficult temperament— commonly referred to as hyperactivity or attention disorder.

This kind of description helps parents understand the extent and nature of their child's problems and to tie these problems to specific situations. If you do not understand, or if you disagree with an assessment, it is important to let the evaluator know. It is the evaluator's obligation to help you understand what is being presented to you.

WHAT DOES THE DIAGNOSIS REALLY MEAN?

The purpose of evaluation is not to label your child or make decisions about a particular treatment (i.e., medication). A diagnosis of hyperactivity does not imply that any particular treatment is necessary. It is also foolish to assume that any single treatment will deal with all the child's problems in all situations. The majority of problems hyperactive children experience cannot be cured but must be managed effectively.

REMEMBER . . .

✦ No single piece of information either confirms or denies the possibility your child may be hyperactive.

✦ There are, however, many behavioral and developmental factors that suggest hyperactivity.

✦ Hyperactive children are inattentive, distractible, impulsive, easily overaroused, restless, and have difficulty delaying rewards.

✦ There is a big difference in the kinds of behavioral problems a hyperactive child may have depending on age.

✦ If you suspect your child may be hyperactive, seek help from your physician, psychologist, or special education team.

✦ The role of the physician is to search for a medical cause of hyperactivity, determine the need for medical testing, and make decisions concerning the need for medical treatment.

✦ A thorough evaluation for hyperactivity includes information concerning your child's history, intelligence, personality, academic achievement, friends, home behavior, school behavior, and medical status.

CHAPTER 3

What Causes Hyperactivity?

Jeremy entered first grade shortly after his sixth birthday. He was impulsive in kindergarten and often interrupted the teacher and other students. His problems were even worse in first grade, and he was unable to sit still. Three years ago, Jeremy had a series of epileptic seizures and his doctor prescribed phenobarbital. He has had no further seizures, but his parents have noticed that he has been more hyperactive and has had more difficulty cooperating with other children since he started the medication. When Jeremy was reevaluated by his physician, concern was expressed that the phenobarbital might be contributing to his hyperactivity. Another anticonvulsant was prescribed and his behavior in school improved dramatically, and he was able to sit still in class. He began paying attention more and was able to interact better with the other students.

"I didn't think it would hurt" or "I forgot" are common ways a hyperactive child explains his behavior. But why does a hyperactive child behave that way? There are two other types of answers. To provide them, we will first look at such causes of hyperactivity as brain injury, epilepsy, medication, diet, lead poisoning, and heredity. Then we will try to understand hyperactive behavior as the result of brain activity.

BIRTH INJURY

A baby's first cry is met with excitement as tangible proof that he has made it through what are probably the most dangerous nine months of human life. To fit through the birth canal, the head must change shape so tremendous forces are applied to the skull during labor and delivery. The bones of the skull act like plates of armor and can move, shift, and even slide over each other to allow the skull to change shape. Inside the skull, the brain is distorted and squeezed. Because the skull leads the way and helps to stretch the birth passage so that the head and the rest of the body can be born, it is easy to see how the brain could be injured during birth. Tiny, delicate blood vessels within the brain, or delicate fibers connecting nerve cells to each other, can be torn by the twisting and stretching of the brain. The brain is not ordinarily subjected to this kind of physical stress at any other time during life. If an abnormality is discovered within the brain of the child, the first place to look for the cause is the possibility of an injury during delivery.

In the 1950s and 1960s, it was popular to believe that the cause of hyperactivity in many children was a birth injury. As an explanation, birth injury satisfied parents' interest in knowing why the child had problems and usually absolved both parents of guilt over their child rearing as the cause. It soon became clear, however, that if birth injury caused hyperactivity, behavior problems might be preventable by taking greater care during delivery. Events surrounding delivery became the source of close legal scrutiny. It became necessary to determine whether problems during labor and delivery were a substantial cause of hyperactivity and to define which markers could be used to determine this.

After careful study, it was found that problems during delivery were much less important as a cause of hyperactivity than we had thought. One of the most surprising discoveries was the failure of the Apgar score, a rating based on tone, color, activity, heart rate, and breathing ability of a newborn, to predict subsequent learning and behavior problems. While it seems reasonable to assume that the sickest babies are the most likely to develop learning and behavior problems, studies of large groups of children show that those with learning and behavior problems were no more likely to have low Apgar scores than those without. Most occurrences, during delivery, and measurements of how healthy the baby appears right after birth, are not helpful in telling us which children will become hyperactive.

Pregnancy is a critical time in the baby's development. If the mother's health is poor during the pregnancy, especially if she has medical problems associated with swelling of the ankles and increased blood pressure (eclampsia) prior to delivery, the baby is more likely to develop behavior and learning problems. This is an especially crucial observation. Even though very few children are hyperactive because of illness during pregnancy, we are again reminded of the importance of good prenatal care.

MEDICAL ILLNESS

A child suffering from the flu who has a running nose, cough, sore throat, and fever, often is inattentive and distracted. This behavior change would not be confused with hyperactivity. The onset is abrupt, the association with other symptoms is clear, and when the illness is over, so are the behavior problems. Very few illnesses produce hyperactivity as the major symptom. Long-term or chronic medical illnesses generally have other characteristic symptoms. Malfunctioning of the heart, liver, kidneys, and pancreas produce specific symptoms that generally overshadow any behavioral change.

The thyroid gland, which lies on either side of the windpipe in the lower neck, produces substances (thyroid hormones) that are necessary for normal physical and mental development. Most children whose thyroid gland produces too much hormone have medical symptoms specific to this problem, including a fast heart rate, moist skin, and jittery, trembling hyperactive behavior. For some children, however, the hyperactivity is the major manifestation of the hyperthyroid state. For these children, reducing the level of thyroid hormone will improve the hyperactivity symptoms.

To help readers understand Sydenham (rheumatic) chorea, we will describe J.M., who is a typical child with this disorder. He is an 8-year-old third grader. Ten days after a bout with a sore throat and fever he began having fidgety movements of his face, shoulders, and legs. Over the next week, this uncontrollable fidgeting worsened to the point where he was unable to feed himself and was barely able to walk. Six weeks later he was back in school, but his teacher and family thought he had not completely returned to normal. The fidgety behavior was better but not gone and he had a difficult time sitting in his seat. He also had difficulty with concentrating in class and frequently forgot to hand in his homework. One year later, these problems had improved only minimally. The family was told J.M. had hyperactivity.

There are several differences between J.M., who has Sydenham chorea, and most hyperactive children. J.M. was not hyperactive prior to the sudden onset of severe symptoms. Sydenham chorea, a form of rheumatic fever, is rarely a cause of hyperactivity, but a child who was normal and then becomes hyperactive should be evaluated carefully to rule out the possibility of an underlying medical illness.

SEIZURE DISORDERS

A 7-year-old was able to keep up well in first grade. Over the past three months, since entering second grade, he has had more difficulty paying attention and following the teacher's directions. He sometimes seems to stare right through her and will continue to stare for 10 or 15 seconds. Sometimes his eyes blink. When he is nervous, these spells can occur two or three times a minute and seem to last only a few seconds. This child has a form of epilepsy which is referred to as petit mal or absence seizures. There is a brief loss of awareness, often associated with eye twitching, usually lasting only a few seconds and occurring many times a day. An electroencephalogram (EEG) gives a clear and distinct pattern of abnormality in children with petit mal or absence epilepsy. Medications are available that can eliminate the seizures and prevent the inattention associated with them.

Absence epilepsy is rarely confused with hyperactivity. The episodes of inattention are usually associated with eye blinking, staring, and sometime twitching of the hands and dropping objects. In rare cases, however, the major symptom of absence epilepsy is inattention and deterioration of schoolwork. If a child with inattention and distractibility has frequent staring spells, especially with eye blinking, absence epilepsy should be considered as a possible cause.

SIDE EFFECTS OF MEDICATION

Phenobarbital, a commonly used medication, is effective for controlling some forms of epilepsy. However, some children may develop severe symptoms of hyperactivity when taking phenobarbital. They will then have a reduction in symptoms when medication is discontinued. One study suggested residual effects on learning six months after the medication was discontinued. Most professionals believe that there is no permanent long-term aggravation of hyperactivity following the use of phenobarbital. Other medications that can aggravate hyperactivity include Dilantin, ephedrine, and theophylline. At one time, Dilantin, an anticonvulsant, was recommended for treatment of childhood hyperactivity, but studies have now shown that the drug may instead aggravate the disorder. Medications for the treatment of asthma, such as ephedrine and theophylline, seem to reduce hyperactive behavior in some children and aggravate it in others, but on the average no change is seen. Individual children may improve or be further impaired in reaction to medications for treatment of asthma.

DIET

Decisions are made every day about food. We are told that eating the wrong foods will lead to vitamin deficiency and eating the right foods will lead to health. In our society, dietary changes are proposed to lessen the risk of cancer and heart disease. Young infants often express hunger by crying. When they have been fed, they become placid, sleepy, and more friendly. It is only natural to suspect that dietary changes might improve behavior abnormalities such as hyperactivity.

Many different dietary substances have been suspected of causing or worsening hyperactivity, and as an extension of this, many claims have been that one or another dietary change will produce dramatic improvements. Such claims are often controversial. Different groups advocate different dietary regimens to control hyperactivity while others believe that no dietary approach can improve behavior. Several varied techniques have been devised for evaluating the effect of diet on hyperactivity.

Psychologist Dr. Keith Conners developed a rating scale (Conner's Parent's and Teacher's Questionnaire, Multi-Health Systems, 1988) that allowed parents and teachers to quantify what he described as hyperkinesis. When behavior can be measured, the effects of two different diets can be compared. After evaluating behavior on a normal diet, he placed all the children on one free of artificial colors and additives. Dr. Conners then used a cookie challenge to separate good and bad diets. Every day the children received a cookie with roughly the same appearance, flavor, and color. On same days, the suspicious substances had been removed from the cookies; on other days they contained a full day's supply of these substances.

While it is difficult to summarize the results of Dr. Conners' studies, he found that many children had improvement in hyperactivity symptoms when they were put on what he describes as a Feingold Diet; one low in artificial colors and food additives. He found, however, that even the children who initially showed improvement on the diet did not regress on the days they were given the loaded cookies. While some believe the initial improvement on the diet shows that it works, most believe the failure of the cookie challenge to reverse the effect shows there is no real improvement as a result of restricting artificial colors and additives.

This kind of study has failed to show any substantial effect of additives, colors, or preseveratives on behavior. In almost every study, if the effect of other influences on behavior is eliminated, no significant deterioration in behavior results from additives, colors, and preseveratives eaten by children, and no improvement in behavior occurs when they are removed.

The effect of dietary sugar on behavior has also been studied. Researchers first quantify a baseline period of behavior. This is followed by a period in which the child is prevented from eating the suspected problem food or the suspected substance is added to the diet. Observation continues without observer or child knowing which diet is being used (double blind). For example, aspartame (Nutrasweet) is an artificial sweetner often used in sugar-free diet tests. Almost without exception these studies have shown no effect of dietary sugar on hyperactive-inattentive behavior.

While it is generally accepted that sugar or additives do not cause hyperactivity, studies using additives and food colors have been criticized for not testing the children with a broad enough range of these substances. Some estimates have suggested that many hyperactive children regularly ingest three to four times the amount of colors and additives usually studied. Others argue the children were given too little processed sugar. There has also been concern that the aspartame used as a sugar substitute might itself cause problems—a phenomenon that would mask improvement gained by eliminating processed sugar.

Despite all the evidence against diet as a cause of hyperactivity, new evidence has changed some researchers' thinking. Among them is Dr. Conners, author of some of the original diet studies, who now concludes that under certain circumstances sugar, or even carbohydrate (a form of sugar molecules), may aggravate hyperactivity. Conners further suggests that other dietary substances, mainly foods rich in protein, may neutralize the effect of sugar. Another group, with some scientific support, believes that if milk, wheat and certain other foods are eliminated along with sugar and additives, some children will respond with decreased hyperactivity.

As it is impossible to prove that an elimination diet *never* produces clinical change, it is difficult to know how much importance to give to the small number of studies that seem to suggest a link between hyperactivity and diet in some children. Nevertheless, it remains generally accepted that diets do not have a significant effect on hyperactivity.

LEAD

Lead is a metal that has no known biological value, but the ingestion of lead can poison the human energy system. When lead was ingested in large quantities by children eating flaking lead paint from the walls of older homes and apartments, lead poisoning, a serious and often fatal condition, occurred. Many children died as a result of swelling of the brain. Some of the children who survived the initial severe episodes developed learning and behavior problems. At first it was suspected that the abnormal behavior may have predated lead exposure. In other words, the children's behavior and learning problems prompted them to eat flaking pieces of paint. However, several other studies have raised questions concerning the effect of lead on learning and behavior.

Children who lived near a lead smelter helped to show that even low levels of lead can cause abnormalities. These children were exposed to lead because of the location of their homes rather than by their actions. When behavior and learning were analyzed, a striking correlation with lead exposure was found. Preexisting behavior could not be blamed for their lead exposure.

Another group of children helped show a further relationship between lead and learning and behavior problems. Thousands of children in the Boston area brought to school their baby teeth that had fallen out. Analysis of these teeth showed that children who had accumulated more lead in their teeth had, on the average, lower IQ's as well as more learning and behavior problems than children with less lead in their teeth. The differences in IQ and other tests were not large but were scientifically reliable.

Once these children with slightly higher lead exposure and slightly lower IQ have been discovered, should they be treated for lead poisoning? No, the treatment would be too dangerous given the small difference in learning. The effort to prevent lead related learning and behavior problems has focused on environmental sources of exposure, including lead in the air from gasoline, and lead in water pipes.

EAR INFECTIONS

Ear infections often cause fussiness, pain, and fever. Hearing loss and speech and language problems are known to result occasionally. Other than the possibility of hearing loss, no permanent problems from ear infections are expected. But when a group of hyperactive children were evaluated, a surprising frequency of ear infections was discovered. More than two thirds of the hyperactive children previously had more than 10 ear infections, while only one in five similar, but not hyperactive, children had had that many.

Before we can conclude that ear infections cause hyperactivity, we must understand that there are other possible explanations. For example, if the hyperactive child was more sensitive to the pain of infection and therefore more likely to be taken to the doctor, this higher frequency of ear infection diagnosis would be the result rather than the cause of the problem behavior. It may also be that hyperactivity and ear infections represent symptoms with a similar neurological cause. Additional study of the relationship between ear infections and hyperactivity will be needed before we can justify considering them a cause.

HEREDITY

The relationship between hyperactivity and heredity has been clearly established. The first heredity link resulted from studying the relatives of hyperactive children. It was learned that a hyperactive child was four times as likely to have other family members with the same problem. However, the relationship between the child and his family contained environmental factors too. The child's behavior problems could have been due to the behavior of his parents. Furthermore, a child with behavior problems might have contributed to a chaotic environment which in turn might have contributed to behavior problems in other family members. Other studies were needed to establish a causal link between hyperactivity and heredity.

To show that the increased incidence of hyperactivity within a family was a function of heredity rather than environment, it was necessary to study situations in which a child was raised away from his biological family. Adopted children provide a group in which the occurrence of hyperactivity is not affected by the everyday influence of the biological family. The hereditary link in hyperactivity was established when it was found that parents and other blood relatives of hyperactive adopted children are four times more likely to have hyperactive behavior.

Another way of studying the effect of heredity is to compare the behavior of the two different types of twins: genetically identical twins, who are the result of the ovum's splitting during conception; and genetically different (fraternal) twins, who are the result of two separate ova. If heredity were important, identical twins would behave more alike than fraternal twins. The observed increase in the occurrence of hyperactivity in identical twins, compared with fraternal twins, is one of the most compelling demonstrations of the hereditary factor as an underlying cause of hyperactivity.

Families with affected children demonstrate a wide range of symptoms, and a child's behavior cannot be predicted from family history alone. Some hyperactive parents have no hyperactive children, while some normal parents have children with severe problems. Many factors determine which children will be hyperactive.

BRAIN INJURY

We have learned a great deal about the effects of brain injury from physicians who have treated battlefield injuries. Head wounds, either from a projectile, fall, or other forceable bump on the head, are not uncommon in wartime. These injuries have provided an opportunity to look at changes in the thinking and behavior resulting from brain injury. Observations of soldiers after head injuries in World War I and World War II represent some of the earliest work on the effect of brain injury on human behavior and thinking. One remarkable finding was that the ability to concentrate and pay attention deteriorates after brain injury regardless of which area of the brain was injured.

It was long thought that each area of the brain had a specific function. According to this reasoning, injury to one area of the brain would result in a decrease or elimination of the brain's ability to carry out only the function controlled by that part of the brain. For example, control of the right hand is believed to be centered in the left frontal part of the brain because an injury here impairs the person's ability to control the right (opposite) hand. Likewise, injury of the occipital, or back part of the brain, on the right side, affects vision to the left. However, injuries to any part of the brain seem to have some effect on the ability to concentrate and pay attention. This nonspecific deterioration became known as the brain injury syndrome. Other forms of brain injury inflicted by stroke (damage to brain tissue from lack of blood flow), multiple sclerosis (loss of protective covering around nerve connections), or encephalitis (attack on brain cells by a viral infection) could also cause changes in attention and concentration similar to those caused by direct injury to the brain. Researchers have demonstrated that a history of brain injury is present in only a very small percentage of hyperactive children.

THE BRAIN MODEL FOR ADHD

The brain appears somewhat like a three-pound boxing glove placed inside the skull with fingers facing the eyes and the thumb below the fingers. The part of the boxing glove closest to the eyes is called the frontal lobe; the knuckles, the parietal lobe; the wrist, the occipital lobe; and the thumb, the temporal lobe. These are the parts of the cerebral hemispheres that sit atop the brain stem and cerebellum. The cerebellum, or balance center, sits between the knuckles and wrist. The wristlike projection from the center of the brain extending toward the feet, is the brain stem, which links the cerebral hemispheres, or thinking part of the brain, with the spinal cord. The finger's width spinal cord runs from the top of the neck through the spinal column, stopping just below the rib cage.

Much of what we know about the function of different parts of the brain comes from observations of people who have suffered accidental injuries. A unique clinical pattern of change results from injury to each area. Injuries to the right side of the brain result in deficiencies or difficulties with the left side of the body. Injuries to the frontal lobes result in inability to use the motor system. Injuries to the parietal lobes result in inability to use the sensory system, and injuries to the occipital lobes result in inability to use the visual system. When the brain stem is damaged, loss of consciousness occurs.

Injuries to some areas can produce changes in behavior bearing some similarity to hyperactivity. For example, injury to the frontal lobes can produce an indifference to the consequences of behavior and sometimes increased impulsiveness. In addition, injury to almost any part of the brain seems to contribute to some decrease in attention and concentration. This observation was the basis for the early belief that hyperactivity was a symptom of brain damage. However, injury or removal of any particular part of the brain does not cause hyperactivity as its major or only symptom.

We have gained insight about brain function from animal studies. Symptoms that resemble hyperactivity have been induced in rats. These hyperactive rats move around more and have difficulty in mazes. They are worse when treated with phenobarbital (a sedative), and improve when treated with amphetamine (a stimulant) in a manner similar to hyperactive children.

These rats develop hyperactivity as a result not of injury to a specific area of the brain but from an injury to a chemical system. Dopamine and noradrenalin are chemicals that are produced in cells within a small area of the brain stem and are then distributed to all areas of the brain through nerve projections called axons. The rats become hyperactive not when the cells are injured within the brain stem, but when the dopamine and noradrenalin nerve endings, which are located throughout the brain far from the cell bodies, are damaged. This prevents the chemicals from being distributed normally to other cells throughout the brain.

These studies suggest the importance of chemical systems that utilize dopamine and noradrenalin. In a simple model, these systems, when intact, help to control hyperactivity, and when they are not working well, hyperactivity results. Cells located in the brain stem may be able to modify behavior by communicating with other cells throughout the brain. The brain can be thought of as a group of electric wires and relay stations. At each relay station, wires from different parts of the brain can come together to influence the next nerve cell.

To relate the brain's complex function to hyperactivity, let us imagine an attention center composed of nerve cells in the brain stem possibly utilizing dopamine. This center can influence many relay points throughout the brain by making them more or less sensitive to input from other cells. Under the direction of this center, the cells of the brain, and thus the child, may become more or less sensitive to outside distractions. He may be more deliberate or more impulsive in his actions, depending on the effect the attention center has on the relay points.

A normal child is able to concentrate, pay attention, and be deliberate in some circumstances while being impulsive, quick thinking, and quick acting in others. The attention center would be working to improve the child's concentration and decrease distractibility while in the classroom so that outside noises and events do not prevent his paying attention and completing his work. However, outside on the playground, quick response to a ball thrown at him with impulsive response is needed to succeed in a baseball game.

This brain model lets us see hyperactive children as having an attention center that is not working well. This dysfunction leads to performance problems. They are often impulsive and act quickly when they should be deliberate. They are often not able to concentrate and finish their work unless it is interesting or outside rewards are offered. One cause of hyperactive behavior can therefore be viewed in terms of a poorly functioning attention center.

The attention center model also helps us to understand the difference between hyperactivity and learning disabilities. A learning disability results from dysfunction within the cerebral hemispheres. Information is not transferred appropriately from one part of the brain to another. For hyperactivity, however, information may be transferred quite efficiently and effectively from one part of the brain to the other, but the dysfunction of the attention center prevents the child from concentrating, paying attention, and controlling his impulses.

Using the attention center model for hyperactivity, parents can understand the cause of hyperactivity in terms of brain function. The attention center can be seen to be affected by both hereditary and environmental factors. Treatments for hyperactivity, both through changes in behavior and medication, can be understood as they affect the attention center deep within the brain.

REMEMBER . . .

✦ Environmental causes, such as brain injury, epilepsy, certain medications, diet, lead poisoning, and heredity have all been implicated in hyperactivity.

✦ Heredity is the most frequent cause of hyperactivity.

✦ Hyperactivity can also be understood as resulting from a dysfunction in the attention center in the brain that prevents the child from concentrating, and controlling activity level, emotions, and planning. Hyperactive behavior, therefore, can be viewed as poor functioning of this attention center leading to performance problems.

PART II

PORTRAIT OF THE HYPERACTIVE CHILD

CHAPTER 4

Is Tim Hyperactive or Just Four Years Old?

Tim's parents have found him to be a difficult and frustrating child. As an infant, Tim was often irritable, overactive, and moody. He had trouble fitting into routines, and his irritable, high-pitched crying caused his parents frequently to curtail family outings. At age four, he continues to be overactive and temperamental, rarely sits still, acts impulsively, and appears to engage in a high degree of risk-taking behavior. This has resulted in numerous bumps, bruises, and half a dozen trips to the hospital emergency room. Tim is extremely aggressive around his brothers and friends. He continues to frustrate easily and has tantrums on a daily basis. His parents have been asked to remove him from two preschools. He provides his parents with very little pleasure, and they are at their wits end: angry, frustrated, and unhappy. They also anticipate that Tim may have serious problems with learning and behavior when he enters kindergarten. Despite all his difficulties though, Tim, too, is aware of his struggles and his parents' unhappiness.

One of the most frequent questions parents ask concerns the age at which hyperactivity can be accurately identified. Early diagnosis and treatment would minimize stress to the child and family and help parents start modifying their lives to better manage the world around their hyperactive child. In the long run, early intervention may go a long way in reducing the wide variety of secondary, behavioral and emotional problems many hyperactive children develop.

We have discussed the four core problems hyperactive children experience, but, as we also noted, each child's problems can vary. Temperamentally difficult 4-year-olds may experience very different problems at home, on the playground, or at preschool.

To accurately identify which young children are showing early signs of hyperactivity, it is important to understand how a specific behavior may look at different ages. For example, authors Dorothea and Sheila Ross (*Hyperactivity: Current Issues, Research and Theory.* 1982, John Wiley & Sons.) have described the process by which the thrashing, temperamental infant could very well become the frantic, overactive preschooler. At school age, this child may be hyperactive, inattentive, and impulsive, leaving many tasks unfinished. By the teenage years, he may be not quite as impulsive or restless but continue to be fidgety, disorganized, and inattentive. Finally, in adulthood, this individual may have difficulty completing tasks and may be overenergetic and disorganized.

Observing a specific behavior from a developmental perspective is also important for an understanding of why adults may overlook a child's particular behavior at one age but may be intolerant of it at another. A restless 4-year-old unable to pay attention may be casually described by the preschool teacher as immature. But a 6-year-old with a similar level of inattentive, restless behavior is usually described by the first-grade teacher as a significant school problem.

Can hyperactivity be identified in very young children? Although the diagnosis is usually reserved for school-age children, studies of younger children have suggested that a number of early developmental factors and behaviors appear to precede hyperactivity. By understanding these issues and behaviors, parents and professionals can identify those children at risk and begin a program of early intervention.

INFANCY

Doctors Stella Chess and Alexander Thomas, psychiatry pioneers and researchers, have spent years researching and chronicling the temperamental patterns of children. Temperament comprises a set of inherited qualities. For example, from the moment of birth, some infants fit into routines very well, others do not; some appear uncomfortable and overwhelmed in new situations, while others do not. These behavior patterns are observed in infants long before their parents have had the opportunity to affect the child's behavior by the way they interact with them. These qualities affect the infant's ability to respond to parent's expectations and behavior. These qualities play a role in determining the manner in which the world responds to the child.

Researchers have consistently identified nine temperamental qualities that all children possess. These vary in intensity from low to moderate to high. For some qualities, such as activity, a low level may be desirable. For others, such as predictability or being able to fit into daily routines, a high level may be good. It is also important to understand that the presence and severity of particular temperamental traits by themselves does not necessarily indicate problems. As discussed in Chapter 1, simply having a high activity level does not mean a child will have significant problems. The nine temperamental traits are activity level, attention span, persistence, ability to deal with change or new experiences, adaptability to change over time, intensity of reaction, predictability of behavior, threshold (what does it take to get this child's attention?), and mood.

Temperamental qualities are neither good nor bad, they simply are. They affect the way your child responds to you and, ultimately, how you respond to your child. A child with an easy temperament characterized by a low activity level, good attention span, and ability to adapt to change, approach new situations, fit into routines, and demonstrate a positive mood, will be easy to raise and result in parents who feel they are quite competent. On the other hand, a child with difficult temperament very quickly results in parents who question their own competency and reasons for having children. Unfortunately, just as the easy child is ultimately perceived as good and normal, the temperamentally difficult child is often perceived as bad and abnormal. These labels are not only inaccurate but further contribute to impaired parent–child relationships.

As author and child psychiatrist Dr. Stanley Turecki has noted, "Some children are born difficult." Approximately 5% to 10% of infants appear to have a difficult temperament. These children do not respond well to changes in their environment. They have greater negative mood and may also have intense reactions to even minor events in their environment.

Difficult infants usually have a very high activity level. They may be restless and overactive in their sleep patterns and a challenge during routine care activities such as changing and bathing. They often have a high-pitched cry. Some parents describe this infant as excessively colicky. Excessive irritability appears to be a better description. These infants seem unhappy most of the time and no particular circumstance seems connected to their unhappiness. These infants also appear to have irregular sleep patterns and have great difficulty settling down to sleep.

Difficult infants are often described as uncooperative in nursing. As Drs. Dorothea and Sheila Ross have noted, these infants may be obstinate, picky, and obstructive feeders. There also appears to be an unexplained higher occurrence of allergy to formula among this group of difficult infants. We do not know whether this is a cause or a consequence of the infant's difficulty.

In some studies, as many as 70% of difficult infants develop school-age problems. Although an infant's temperament can change as the child matures, these difficulties responding to the world appear stable. For example, one study found that toddlers with a frequent negative mood and very intense reactions to events in their environment were at significantly greater risk for elementary school problems than toddlers who had more positive mood and less intense reactions to minor events.

Are all these infants with difficult temperament hyperactive? *No!* These early signs of developmental difficulty are nonspecific in predicting exactly the type of later problems these children may experience. Difficult infants, as they grow, appear as a group to have more problems with learning, behavior, socialization, hyperactivity, and inattention than other infants. Some may experience a combination of these problems. Some, however, pass through the period of difficult infancy and do not progress to later childhood problems. As such, this temperamentally difficult infant population appears best described as *at risk* for later difficulty.

The temperamentally difficult infant is difficult to parent effectively. New parents may feel guilty due to their inability to calm or comfort this child. In some situations, this results in overly permissive or solicitous behavior on the part of the parent. In response, the child is further impaired in developing any sense of self-control.

Other parents may feel angry and consciously or unconsciously reject this child. Many years ago, Dr. D. W. Winnicott wrote that most mothers are good enough for most children. The temperamentally difficult infant is a challenge to even the best and most competent parents.

Although the most obvious pattern of extraordinary temperament is the difficult child, many temperamental qualities can interact and cause differences in childhood behavior. For example, the child often described as shy usually is overwhelmed in new situations, does not adapt well to change, and may have a low threshold of tolerance so that even minor events are disturbing. It is also easy to understand, based on this example, how the interaction of any two temperament variables either creates a greater problem or results in one factor acting as an insulator for another. For example, a child with a low threshold of tolerance but a fairly low reaction intensity may be bothered by many things going on about him, but will not have much of a behavioral problem when distressed. On the other hand, a child with a low threshold but high reaction intensity will make everyone around well aware of his unhappiness.

Parenting any child requires time and effort. It is not an easy task. The difficult infant, however, may frustrate, anger, and irritate parents because of the child's inability to respond to parents as expected. As adults, we hold certain expectations concerning how children should behave. When they do not, we blame them, ourselves, or both. This process most certainly has a negative impact on bonding and the type of relationship this child and parents are able to develop. An impaired parent–child relationship will have a lasting negative effect on this child.

Unfortunately, studies have suggested that a poor parent–child relationship is frequently observed in the histories of children diagnosed with temperamental and behavioral problems. At the time of diagnosis with young children, it is often difficult, if not impossible, to determine how much of the child's problems stem from poor or inappropriate parenting and how much actually stems from difficult temperament.

PRESCHOOLERS

During the preschool years, children learn a tremendous amount about themselves and their world. It has been suggested by medical researchers that the preschool child's brain is supercharged and contains more brain cell connections than at any other time in life. Normal attention and activity level in toddlers and preschoolers is very difficult to define. What is considered normal or acceptable varies. With younger children, it is much more difficult to identify that arbitrary line at which the child's behavior is problematic.

Dr. Susan Campbell, researcher and author of a textbook about behavior problems in preschool children (*Behavior Problems in Preschool Children,* Guilford Press, 1990) provides an illuminating description of the normal 3-year-old. The typical, age-appropriate behavior of this child may be vigorous, unrestrained, and capricious. Three-year-olds demonstrate curiosity, exploration, and boundless energy; they attend readily to new stimulation in their environment and are frequently unrestrained, enthusiastic, and exuberant. It is, therefore, very difficult to determine when young children's pattern of behavior crosses the invisible line that suggests they are overactive, impulsive, and inattentive to what professionals would consider a clinically significant degree.

In addition, with young children, parental knowledge, temperament, and ability to tolerate the child's behavior are critical variables. It will determine how vehemently the parents complain and how powerful they may be in further negatively influencing this child's behavior. Overly rigid parents who may not understand that 3-year-olds cannot sit still for long periods of time could create a little monster by repeated harassing, haranguing, and punishing their child for not sitting still. On the other hand, parents who understand normal 3-year-old behavior and in fact are able to tolerate even excessive behaviors, such as a high activity level, go a long way in reducing the secondary negative impact this level of activity may have on the child's emotional and behavioral development.

There has also been a trend in psychology that problems of preschool children are not serious. It has long been thought that problems of young children reflect stages the child may be passing through, rather than the early signs of what could become a lifetime disorder. With regard to hyperactivity, ignoring these early signs, especially when they last more than 12 months, and in the absence of specific information suggesting the child's problems are caused by poor parenting or other life difficulties, results in the loss of valuable treatment time. Treatments involving the child in a structured preschool program, teaching prosocial and problem solving skills, and providing parents with ideas to improve the child's behavior at home, go a long way toward avoiding and minimizing the many secondary problems hyperactive children develop.

Many difficult infants become difficult toddlers and preschoolers. At least 70% to 80% of children later identified as hyperactive could have been identified by parental history by age four. Research by Dr. Barry Garfinkel, at the University of Minnesota, suggests that based on parental history, the majority of children later identified as hyperactive could have been identified at as early as one and a half years.

Toddlers and preschoolers demonstrating the early signs of hyperactivity also appear to have a higher rate of language disorders. In some studies, as high as 50% to 70% of young hyperactive children experienced receptive or expressive language problems. It is unclear if the child's difficult temperament contributes to delayed language or delayed language contributes to the child's difficult temperament. Researchers have also suggested that the hyperactive child has difficulty making the transition from tactile stimulation, to verbal and visual stimulation. Infants learning about the world before they acquire language and the ability to attach verbal labels to things must touch, feel, and taste as a means of gaining information. Once effective language is established, words replace touch. Typically, hyperactive preschoolers continue to need to touch and feel things possibly as a means of gaining sensory input from their world.

In his long-term studies, Dr. Walter Mischel has found a most interesting relationship between the ability to wait for rewards, language skills, and success as a teenager and young adult. Dr. Mischel took a group of preschool children, gave each of them a snack and asked them to wait a period of time before eating the snack. Some of the children were able to wait, some ate the snack immediately. He then gave all the children a second snack and informed them that if they could wait a period of time he would reward them with additional snacks. Again, the very same children immediately ate their single snack while the others were able to wait to earn additional snacks.

Dr. Mischel discovered that the children able to wait talked to themselves and convinced themselves that waiting was worthwhile. The children who could not wait simply did not utilize these verbal strategies. He followed both groups of children as they grew up. As teenagers, the group that was able to delay eating the snack was doing significantly better in many areas, including academic achievement, college entrance exams, and general behavior compared with the group that could not wait. While the snack test is certainly not a clinical test, and for a single child would not be expected to accurately predict much about the child's future behavior, this line of research is important. It helps us understand the relationship between language, the ability to wait for rewards, and future success. Hyperactive children, unfortunately, appear to have greater language problems and one of their core problems is an inability to delay gratification.

As neither the threat of punishment nor the promise of reward has an impact on the child's behavior, this often creates a marked degree of family stress and tension. While this is frustrating for parents, it is important to stop for a moment to understand that these are problems of difficult temperament and incompetence rather than noncompliance.

Finally, it has been suggested that approximately one out of five preschool children experience some type of problem with social development. Unfortunately, almost all hyperactive preschoolers are reported as experiencing some form of social problem. The social problems of hyperactive children will be described in greater depth in the next chapter.

WHAT SHOULD PARENTS DO?

In summary, it appears that there is significant scientific literature to suggest that by evaluating certain temperamental factors and behaviors in infants (activity level, irritability, sleep, feeding, mood, etc.) and others in preschoolers (activity level, language, attention span, mood, parent behavior, etc.), we can identify a group of children who appear to be greater risk of being diagnosed as hyperactive in childhood. The problems many of these young children are experiencing usually do not represent transient or short-term developmental stages. Usually they will not be outgrown. These may be the early signs of what will become, for many children, a chronic behavior disorder.

Ignoring these early signs of hyperactivity represents a mistake on the part of parents and our medical and clinical community. While early intervention will not cure hyperactivity or difficult temperament, it will go a long way toward minimizing the long list of secondary problems that hyperactive children develop.

WHAT CAN AND SHOULD BE DONE?

We would like to see pediatricians and family practitioners routinely screening infant temperament. They can identify those infants with difficult temperament and provide parents with resources. Such parental education might include something as simple as reading a book, such as Dr. Turecki's text, *The Difficult Child,* (Bantam Books, 1985) ideas for effective management at home, and even referral into a parent–infant training program. This will help parents of temperamentally difficult infants cope more effectively with the child as well as with their own frustrations. The goal of these interventions is to increase your competence. Thus, skill, patience, and tolerance will diffuse the development of long-term emotional and behavioral problems in your child. On the other hand, if you become angry, irritated, anxious, and confused concerning your inability to manage your child, it will certainly worsen problems. The daily interaction between you and your young child is critical in determining the long-term outcome of your child's personality and behavior.

Preschool teachers can and should be trained to identify toddlers and preschoolers at risk not only for problems of hyperactivity but for the early signs of learning disabilities and other psychological disorders such as those related to anxiety and depression. In addition, specialized preschool programs funded by the federal government, should be supported by the community. These programs can help at-risk children begin to meet the demands of our society and prepare them to be integrated successfully into school.

Finally, the professional community should make a concerted effort to effectively educate *all* parents concerning temperament, childhood behavior, and ways to cope with variations in behavior.

Parents can be helped to understand that weaknesses in attention, impulse control, and activity level in and of themselves are not always problems. They create problems when we do not understand them, make inappropriate or excessive demands, and fail to help these children in constructive ways.

REMEMBER . . .

✦ Infants, toddlers, and preschoolers with difficult temperament appear at significantly greater risk of developing later childhood problems.

✦ The majority of children later identified as hyperactive exhibited difficult temperament during infancy, preschool, and toddler years.

✦ The young child with difficult temperament exhibits a high activity level, poor attention, intense reactions to changes in the environment, a low threshold, more negative mood, and difficulty fitting into routines.

✦ A high percentage of children with hyperactivity also appear to experience language problems.

✦ Parents' ability to understand and effectively manage difficult temperament makes a significant and positive impact on the present and future level of behavioral problems the child exhibits.

CHAPTER 5

Are Friends an Impossible Dream for the Hyperactive Child?

Judy and Paul both suffer from hyperactivity. They are inattentive, restless, impulsive, and easily distracted; completing work at school and at home is difficult. But despite the similarity in their hyperactivity, they experience different social problems. Judy is unable to make friends. Although she very much wants to have them, she appears unable to say the right thing or to approach other children at just the right moment. Her attempts at joining others for activities often results in her interrupting what is going on. Judy is not very popular. She is not feared or disliked but simply lacks basic social skills and so is not sought out by other children. Paul on the other hand is able to make friends. He just can't keep them. He shares the same interests as other children and is able to join an activity or share in conversation. However, due to his impulsive, easily frustrated style, inevitably during games or other activities with friends, he loses his temper. He attempts to control and dominate play activities, which often results in fights. Other children have begun actively to avoid playing with him. He has worked his way through all the available friends and has even played with some younger neighborhood children. At this point, however, none of the children appear willing to tolerate his aggressive, controlling behavior.

Judy and Paul exhibit the most common social problems of hyperactive children. Some, like Judy, exhibit behavior that is not terrible but results in a lack of social graces. Other hyperactive children like Paul, exhibit behavior that is aggressive and domineering. While this aggressive behavior does not occur very often, when it occurs, other children quickly become intolerant. Both Judy and Paul desperately long for social contact yet they seem unable to understand the impact their behavior has on others, to learn new skills or to change their inefficient behavior so that they can achieve social success.

Over the past 10 years, mental health professionals and educators have taken a new interest in the area of social skills and friendship development. Numerous books and programs have been developed, and it is now well recognized that a child's ability to develop and maintain friendships is an essential component of sound mental health, and is an important predictor of that child's happiness even into adulthood.

Friendships are developed and maintained through play. Researchers and theorists over the past 40 years have emphasized the importance of play as a means by which children learn to control their environment effectively and strengthen thinking and social skills. Further, pretend play, which all normal children engage in beginning at about 12 months, is considered a very important developmental milestone for normal personality. Play not only enhances the child's contacts with the world but helps the child develop an appropriate self-image as well. Some research studies have suggested that children who are able to play effectively with others experience fewer childhood problems.

By preschool age, pretend play is a frequent activity in helping children develop the basic foundations for normal social development. At-risk or hyperactive preschoolers, because of their inattentive, impulsive behavior, may be deprived of these interactions and thus fail to begin to take the steps necessary for appropriate social development.

Older hyperactive children have great difficulty developing friends and more complex social skills because of their inattentive, impulsive, and overcharged style. Social problems, unfortunately, are frequently overlooked when considering the difficulties hyperactive children experience. Some researchers have found, however, that problems with friends may be as efficient a way of identifying hyperactive children as are problems with attention span, impulsivity, and overactivity.

Observations of the hyperactive child's social problems on the part of teachers and parents frequently include fighting, interrupting others, and being more disliked than other children. A study by Dr. Russell Barkley, published in 1981, found that 80% of parents of hyperactive children reported their children were having serious problems playing with other children. Such problems occur in less than 10% of normal children. Hyperactive teenagers and adults with histories of hyperactivity also report problems with friends. In fact, it has been suggested that social problems for hyperactive children increase with age.

Children of all ages quickly become aware of the hyperactive child's behavior and tend to view this child in a negative light. Often this leads to rejection that can foster even more problems. The frustration of being rejected often results in an increase of aggression and attempts to control friends. It is important to recognize that many hyperactive children are disliked by their playmates. Doctors William Pelham and Michael Milich suggested in 1984 that hyperactive children differ from other children in their social interactions. Hyperactive children demonstrate excessive behaviors (i.e., hitting) that result in rejection and social skills deficits (i.e., not understanding how to start a conversation) that result in not being accepted socially. At school, hyperactive children are reported to be more negative in word and deed. Unfortunately, the hyperactive child is least able to cope with the frustration of peer rejection and often a vicious cycle develops. In response to rejection, the hyperactive child attempts to exert more control over other children. This results in more misbehavior and further rejection. This happens both in the classroom and on the playground.

Although hyperactive children may have more negative interaction with friends, they also may have just as much interaction as other children. Some also have just as much positive interaction. However, since children usually judge their self-worth in terms of the opinions of others, rejection by friends, as noted by authors Dorothea and Sheila Ross, results in lowered self-esteem for the hyperactive child. This leads to even greater problems since these difficulties further restrict the hyperactive child's opportunities to develop and practice appropriate social skills.

Within the two broad types of social skill problems hyperactive children experience, researchers have attempted to identify specific skill weaknesses that may be common for these children. It has been suggested that the hyperactive child, however, experiences such a wide range of social problems that identifying any specific behavioral or skill weakness has been almost impossible. Parents and teachers describe social difficulties of the hyperactive child, including off-task behavior, disruptive behavior, impulsiveness, immaturity, aggressive problem solving, and difficulty with basic communication. Hyperactive children also have difficulty adapting to new situations. Given the range of situations hyperactive children are placed in, as well as marked differences in parents, teachers, siblings, and demands of various settings, it is not surprising that a specific, single pattern of social difficulty has not been identified as common to all hyperactive children.

More than any other social problem, parents, teachers, friends, and siblings of hyperactive children complain about aggressive behavior. Researchers have suggested that aggression is a stable trait. This means that younger children who are aggressive usually continue to be aggressive as they grow older. It is unclear whether this pattern of behavior is inherited, acquired because of ineffective coping methods on the part of parents and professionals, or most likely, a combination of both.

Aggression is not one of the basic factors in the diagnosis of hyperactivity. It is, however, a frequent component in the behavior problems hyperactive children exhibit. It has been estimated that at least 30% to 40% of hyperactive children exhibit aggressive, social behavior.

Aggressive behavior has also been found to be a negative predictor in a child's ability to respond to traditional treatments for hyperactivity. Researchers have found that nonaggressive and normal children experience increased social acceptance as they get older, while their hyperactive and aggressive classmates appear to be rejected even more in the higher grades. Other researchers have found that the more problems the hyperactive child has with restlessness, overactivity, and impulsiveness the greater likelihood that child will also have problems with aggression.

What skills do hyperactive children lack to cause this pattern of social problems? Is it simply inattention, impulsiveness, and overactivity that interfere with social relations? Are there certain skills that do not develop because this child does not pay attention very well? As we discussed, researchers have been unable to provide specific answers to these questions. One recent study suggested that inattentive and hyperactive children do not know how to engage in rough play appropriately. They are often unable to make positive statements toward others (i.e., "I like the way you did that") and appropriate verbal requests (i.e., saying "please" instead of "give me that."). These may be three important skills that cause the hyperactive child to be unsuccessful socially. These three skills may also separate hyperactive children: those with and those without friends.

It is also likely that as the result of their inattentive, impulsive style, hyperactive children may not learn how to take someone else's perspective or label emotions effectively. This may interfere with their ability to socialize. However, cause and effect for these problems has not been proven. It is not clear whether this type of cognitive problem leads to, or is the result of, disturbed social relationships.

Is there any hope? Can hyperactive children maintain and keep friends? Researchers have demonstrated that with a combination of stimulant medication, positive reinforcement, and a method known as self-instruction training (learning how to solve problems effectively), hyperactive children can display almost normal levels of both appropriate and inappropriate social behavior. To be effective, such a social skill-building program must help the hyperactive child learn and use appropriate social skills daily; provide rewards for improved behavior; and follow the hyperactive child for a long period of time with booster sessions as needed. Can parents provide some of these skill-building activities? Absolutely!

HELPING YOUR CHILD MAKE AND KEEP FRIENDS

Helping your child make and keep friends is a multistep process. While professional intervention is usually an essential component in this process, parents have many opportunities to interact with their child and play a valuable role. Parents often act as facilitators when they follow through with strengthening the skills taught to their children and the recommendations of the professional. In Step 1, you must help your child learn and use a logical means of solving social problems. In Step 2, you must identify specific areas of skill weakness and attempt, by using the problem-solving model, to help the child strengthen weak skills. Finally in Step 3, you must help the child develop new friendships and make opportunities available for those friendships to grow.

STEP 1: A PROBLEM-SOLVING MODEL

The following problem-solving model was first developed by two social psychologists Drs. M. B. Shure and G. Spivack. It has been adjusted, adapted, and modified, and appears in different versions in many different professional and parent texts. The following is a simplified, four-part version of this model. It can be successfully used for social and for most other problems children experience.

Part 1: Defining the Problem

Due to their impulsiveness and lack of attention, hyperactive children are usually unaware of the impact their behavior has on friends. Thus, the hyperactive child usually denies that his behavior bothers others or that his behavior in any way has contributed to his social problems. It is important to keep this in mind when attempting to teach your hyperactive child a problem-solving model. You must increase your child's social awareness. You are not going to convince your child that he has a problem if he is unable to recognize and understand his behavior. Therefore, it is best to start with a social problem your child recognizes and is willing to accept. Even the most impulsive, hyperactive, oppositional child will accept responsibility for some aspect of his behavior. Use this problem to teach the model rather than starting with a problem that is observed by others rather than by the child.

First help your child develop sensitivity to the problem. While this step may appear obvious, parents and teachers frequently take this for granted. It is usually assumed by adults that since they understand and have accurately defined the problem, the child should agree with this analysis. This is usually not the case. If you and your child do not agree on the source of a problem, a solution is next to impossible.

Your hyperactive child's definition of the problem may be very different from yours. You must patiently work with your child to reach some agreement concerning the problem. For example, if your child is unable to cooperate with a friend, the child's explanation of the problem may be, "He won't agree with me." Your observation of this situation may be just the opposite, that your child is "not playing cooperatively." First, sit down with the child and make a list of all the possible explanations for the problem. This list might include the possibility that the other child wants to be the boss, your child wants to be the boss, the two children have difficulty taking turns being the leader, and so on.

At that point, try to help your child compromise and agree on the most likely explanation of the problem. It is possible that the most likely explanation may include a number of components, such as that neither your child nor his friend are willing to cooperate on this particular issue.

Part 2: What Should Be Done?

In this part, you and your child must identify a variety of possible solutions. Do not expect your child to immediately generate a long list of solutions. Hyperactive children are often unable to generate more than one because they have difficulty dividing their attention. Their solution is likely to be fairly self-centered and will not go very far toward a useful resolution.

Don't lecture your child! Continue to provide other suggestions. Make a written list of all the possible solutions. Even go so far as to suggest humorous solutions to encourage your child's participation. Humor can be a valuable tool in helping the hyperactive child feel comfortable and not threatened during the process.

Part 3: Pick the Best Solution and Think It Through

At this point, you and your child must choose the solution which seems most likely to achieve success. Take the child through each step. In this case, the solution may be that the hyperactive child and his friend will take turns making decisions with each having a chance to be the boss. Help your child understand the steps necessary to achieve success if this is chosen.

In some situations, your hyperactive child may insist on a solution that you do not believe is best. Here, do not debate him about the choice. Try and help him see this through by raising potential problems. If the child refuses to compromise, it may be worthwhile to help the child work through the solution he has chosen, and proceeding to Part 4, allow the child to observe the success or failure of the choice.

Part 4: Is This Working?

At this point, help your child understand what will happen day in and day out with friends if this particular solution works. This may help your hyperactive child develops a sense of cause and effect. Understanding cause and effect is an essential skill for social success. This model may also help your child understand that his behavior is not a series of isolated, unrelated events.

Once the child has had the opportunity to test and practice the solution with you, it is time to try the solution in the real world. When a play session has been completed, it is worthwhile discussing whether the solution was effective. In this way, the child develops the ability to define problems and implement solutions as well as evaluate their success or failure.

Many parents comment that this seems like a very simple (almost too simple) model. That is absolutely *true*. The fact of the matter is that most children independently and intuitively develop the ability to use such a model by age five. Unfortunately, the majority of hyperactive children do not. When faced with social, academic, or other problems in their lives, they respond in an impulsive, nonthinking manner. Without direct instruction, they seem to lack the ability to develop an effective set of skills to solve problems. By repeatedly demonstrating problem solving to your children through the use of this model they will eventually begin to use it independently.

STEP 2: UNDERSTANDING, DEFINING, AND HELPING YOUR CHILD WITH SOCIAL SKILLS WEAKNESSES

The majority of social problems hyperactive children experience are the result of incompetence and not necessarily noncompliance. This is a very important issue. As we discussed in earlier chapters, if a child lacks the ability to perform a certain task, punishment is not an effective intervention for improving that child's performance. This dilemma is especially true when it comes to the social skill problems of hyperactive children. Out of frustration, parents and teachers frequently punish the hyperactive child for both social skill deficiency and inappropriate behavior. In the long run, it creates more frustration and unhappiness for all concerned.

Researchers have identified a number of social skills that are important for making and keeping friends. You can use the following brief questionnaire to evaluate these skills in your hyperactive child. If such a questionnaire was not completed during your child's hyperactivity evaluation, take a few moments and complete it now. It is not meant to be scored but rather to help you identify your child's specific skills weaknesses. Each of these skills will then be further defined, and you will learn how to use the problem-solving model to teach these skills to your child.

SOCIAL SKILLS QUESTIONNAIRE

	My child:		
	is poor at this skill	exhibits this skill as well as others	exhibits this skill better than others
Meeting new people.	_____	_____	_____
Beginning a conversation.	_____	_____	_____
Listening during a conversation.	_____	_____	_____
Ending a conversation.	_____	_____	_____
Joining an ongoing activity with others.	_____	_____	_____
Asking questions appropriately.	_____	_____	_____
Asking for a favor appropriately.	_____	_____	_____
Seeking help from peers appropriately.	_____	_____	_____
Seeking help from adults appropriately.	_____	_____	_____
Sharing.	_____	_____	_____
Interpreting body language.	_____	_____	_____
Playing a game successfully.	_____	_____	_____
Suggesting an activity to others.	_____	_____	_____
Working cooperatively.	_____	_____	_____
Offering to help others.	_____	_____	_____
Saying thank you.	_____	_____	_____
Giving a compliment.	_____	_____	_____
Accepting a compliment.	_____	_____	_____
Apologizing.	_____	_____	_____
Understanding the impact his behavior has on others.	_____	_____	_____

SOCIAL SKILLS QUESTIONNAIRE (continued)

	My child:		
	is poor at this skill	exhibits this skill as well as others	exhibits this skill better than others
Demonstrating the ability to understand other's behavior.	——	——	——
Rewards self.	——	——	——
Follows directions.	——	——	——
Understanding the impact his behavior has on others.	——	——	——
Demonstrating the ability to understand other's behavior.	——	——	——
Comments: _____			

From S. Goldstein and E. Pollock. *Problem Solving Skills Training for Attention Deficit Children.* Copyright, 1988, by Neurology, Learning and Behavior Center. Used by permission of the authors.

The following is a description of each of the skills, why they are important, and the steps you must teach your child if the skill is to be acquired and successfully used.

Skill: Listening to Others

The child's ability to listen to others and acknowledge that he has heard what they have said is essential for problem solving and maintaining friendships. To develop this skill, the child must:

1. Face the person who is speaking and make eye contact.
2. Not speak when others are speaking.

3. Think about what is being said.

4. Be able to take turns when speaking.

Skill: Meeting New People

First impressions are very important. A child's ability to meet someone new and do so in an appropriate fashion, forms an impression on the other individual. To meet someone effectively, the child must learn to introduce himself. To do this, the child must:

1. Decide if he wants to meet this person.

2. Choose an appropriate time to make an introduction.

3. Walk up to the person.

4. Look at the individual.

5. Say his name.

6. Wait for the person to tell him his or her name and ask the person if he or she doesn't tell him.

7. Tell the person something about himself or what he would like to do.

Skill: Starting a Conversation

It is important for children to understand when it is appropriate to start conversations and how to do so. Successful conversational skills require that the child:

1. Decide whom to talk to.

2. Know when to talk.

3. Show interest in a topic the other person might be interested in.

4. Begin speaking in a friendly way.

5. Stay on the topic.

6. Listen to what the other person says.

7. Ask questions.

Skill: Ending a Conversation

Hyperactive children leave many things unfinished—conversations, games, and other social interactions. Knowing how to end an interaction, such as a conversation, is very important. To successfully end a conversation, the child must:

1. Decide why the conversation is to be ended.
2. Decide when to end the conversation.
3. Choose what to say so as not to insult the other person.
4. Wait until the other person stops talking.
5. State what he has to say to end the conversation in a friendly way.

Skill: Self-Reward

One of the authors once opened a fortune cookie and found a fortune that said, "Self-reward is the secret to success." The ability to pat oneself on the back and to recognize and acknowledge self-accomplishments to essential for social success. To be a good self-rewarder, the child must:

1. Decide if a reward is deserved.
2. Tell himself he had done a good job and consider ways to reward himself.
3. Select the best way to reward himself.
4. Reward himself as soon as is *reasonably* possible.

Skill: Asking

Asking questions, seeking help, or requesting a favor all require approaching another individual in a manner that makes the other individual want to respond positively. To ask for things appropriately, the child must:

1. Decide what to ask for.
2. Decide whom to ask.
3. Plan how to ask at an appropriate time.
4. Rehearse what to say.
5. Choose an appropriate time.
6. Get the other person's attention.
7. Tell the person what he needs in a friendly manner.
8. Compromise if he can't get what he wants.
9. Always say thank you.

Skill: Following Instructions

Hyperactive children have difficulty following instructions, usually because they do not pay attention long enough to obtain the instructions. In social situations this usually leads to disaster and rejection by peers. Hyperactive children need to learn to listen effectively and follow instructions. To follow instructions the child must:

1. Listen to what is being said.
2. Ask questions about the topic until it is clear what is being requested.
3. Repeat the instructions to himself (rehearsal).
4. Complete the task one step at a time in the order the instructions have been given.

Skill: Sharing

Hyperactive children, due to their impulsive need to be immediately gratified, often have difficulty sharing. It is not that they are malicious or egocentric, it is simply that their need to reward themselves overwhelms their ability to stop and realize that others are entitled to rewards also. Children who have difficulty sharing very quickly alienate all their friends. To share effectively, a child must:

1. Recognize that sharing is important to keep friends.
2. Decide if he has something to share.
3. Decide with whom he wants to share it.
4. Choose the best time to share.
5. Share in an honest way and not barter or expect something in return when he shares.

Skill: Understanding Body Language

Nonverbal messages often convey quite a bit of information from one friend to another, and often are more subtle than what the child actually says. Therefore, they require even better attention. To read body language effectively, a child must:

1. Face the other person and watch him or her.
2. Look at the person's face.
3. Attempt to identify how the person feels through his or her facial expressions.
4. Look at the individual's body and posture.
5. Identify how the individual may be feeling by his or her posture.
6. If unsure how the individual feels by what is being observed, ask.

Skill: Playing a Game

Playing games by the rules is a mainstay of social activity. Children who cannot play by the rules or leave games unfinished are excluded quickly from games. To play a game effectively, the child must:

1. Understand all the rules of the game.
2. Be willing to review the rules before the game starts.
3. Decide who will play the game.

4. Decide who will start, go second, etc.

5. Be able to wait his turn.

6. Think about how he's playing while he's playing.

7. When the game is over, say something positive to the other players.

Skill: Suggesting an Activity

Hyperactive children often have good ideas for social activities. Unfortunately, their timing if often poor. When they suggest one activity, the other children may be in the middle of another. The hyperactive child may then attempt to bully or force the other children to change activities. To successfully suggest an activity a child must:

1. Decide on an activity he wants to do.

2. Decide with whom he could do the activity.

3. Select the individuals he wants to participate in the activity.

4. Evaluate what is happening at that moment and wait for the right time to approach the others.

5. Recognize that if other children are in the middle of another activity, it might be best to suggest what could be done next.

6. Decide what to say.

7. Decide when to say it.

8. Say things in a friendly way.

9. If the answer is no, be willing to compromise.

Skill: Working Cooperatively

The hyperactive child's impulsive need to be immediately rewarded often overwhelms a willingness to be cooperative. To work cooperatively, a child must:

1. Decide what he wants to do.

2. Decide how he wants to work.

3. State his position.

4. Be a good listener while others state their positions.

5. Be willing to compromise.

6. Act thoughtfully and respect others.

Skill: Offering Help

The remaining skills let others know the child understands how they feel, and what they want or need. One of the best ways to make a friend is to be a good friend by helping others. To offer someone help, the child must:

1. Decide if someone needs help.

2. Decide if that individual wants help.

3. Think of what he could do to help.

4. Decide how to ask if he can help.

5. Choose the best time to offer help.

6. Offer his help.

7. Accept the person's decision either to have him help or not.

Skill: Saying Thank You

Giving positive feedback in the form of thanks and compliments differentiates socially successful from unsuccessful hyperactive children. To say thank you effectively, a child must:

1. Decide if someone did something he wants to thank them for.

2. Decide ways to thank them.

3. Choose the best way to thank the person.

4. Choose the best time to thank the person.

5. Thank them in a friendly way.

6. Tell them why he is thanking them.

Skill: Offering a Compliment

To compliment effectively, the child must:

1. Decide what he wants to tell someone.
2. Decide how he wants to say it.
3. Choose the best time to say it.
4. Choose a good place to say it.
5. Offer the compliment in a friendly way.

Skill: Accepting a Compliment

This is similar to the skills necessary for saying thank you. The child must:

1. Recognize when he is being complimented.
2. Be willing to acknowledge and accept the compliment.
3. Say thank you.

Skill: Apologizing

Because of their impulsive, inattentive style, hyperactive children often do not understand the impact their behavior has on others and therefore rarely apologize. To apologize effectively, a child must:

1. Decide if their behavior requires an apology.
2. Think of ways to apologize.
3. Choose the best way to apologize.
4. Choose the best time to apologize.
5. Choose the best place to apologize.
6. Apologize in an honest way.

Skill: Understanding How His Behavior Affects Others

Just the other week, a young hyperactive child expressed his frustration because he could not understand why another child in line had hit him. During the course of the conversation, it became apparent. The hyperactive child explained that he had been standing on another child's foot but had not realized it and he did not respond when asked to move. The offended child then hit him. Unfortunately, the hyperactive child could not understand that standing on someone's foot would provoke a negative response. To effectively understand the impact his behavior has on others, the child must:

1. Decide which behaviors are important to him.
2. Be aware of how he is behaving.
3. Stay in control of his behavior.
4. State his position if he chooses to behave in a certain way.
5. Think about how others feel because of the way he behaves.
6. Think about what others might say or do because of the way he behaves.
7. Be willing to compromise if his behavior is not accepted by others.

Skill: Empathy

The ability to understand how others feel is essential if a child is to be a good friend. To understand how others feel, he must stop and think about it. To understand other's feelings, the child must:

1. Listen to what others have to say.
2. Watch what other people are doing.
3. Consider the reasons for what a person may be saying or feeling.

4. Consider the best possible explanations for the individual's behavior or comments.

5. Decide if he needs to say or do anything in response.

6. Follow through.

Many of these skills can be reviewed with a child and practiced by role playing. You and the child each choose a part and act out how you might behave, using both appropriate and inappropriate skills. Remember, practicing a skill once or twice is not enough for the child to master that skill. Many hyperactive children understand and can demonstrate appropriate social skills and behavior in well-controlled, quiet, one-on-one settings. Unfortunately, out in the world where emotions run high and there are many distractions, the child's impulsive, nonthinking behavior overwhelms his ability to stop and use the skills he has learned. One way to deal with this problem is to watch your child casually as he is playing with a friend and offer assistance, suggestions, and interventions when problems occur.

Social skills training groups led by professionals will provide numerous opportunities for interaction and intervention. Also be aware of the possibility that other developmental problems such as language difficulties or emotional problems such as anxiety may make learning social skills even more difficult for some hyperactive children. For these children, a professionally led social skills group is essential. It is also important to realize that some children are resistant to working on these skills with parents. Do not attempt to force-feed your child social skills building. This will only lead to further negative reinforcement and very little change in behavior.

STEP 3: OPPORTUNITY

Friends are important. If your child is having difficulty making and keeping friends, it may be helpful to provide supervised opportunities when the child can invite one friend to engage in an enjoyable, reinforcing activity. Help your child find a particular hobby or interest and reinforce participation in that activity. It is important for the hyperactive child to identify something that he does well and can use as a self-esteem building exercise.

Suggestions for Dealing with Aggression

As we have discussed, aggression is not a diagnostic symptom of hyperactivity, but a significant group of hyperactive children have aggression problems. Some children seem prone to using aggression as a means of solving problems. One 2-year-old may have a temper tantrum and throw himself down, crying, and screaming, while another may look around for the most convenient person to bite. While clashes with siblings, friends, and parents occur for all children, the aggressive child takes these to extreme. The impulsive, easily frustrated, hyperactive and aggressive child is quickly provoked and often responds aggressively.

What can be done to reduce aggression? Many parents comment that hyperactive children who respond well to stimulant medication demonstrate fewer aggressive outbursts. This usually occurs because the child has a greater tolerance for frustration. Unfortunately, when these children eventually do get frustrated, they usually continue to use aggression to solve problems. Therefore, you may reduce their outbursts with medication but you must also teach the child a better way of handling conflicts and frustration. For children with numerous and serious outbursts, the help of a qualified professional is essential. Parents can start the process by not using aggressive behavior themselves (i.e., do not hit the TV when it does not work) and by not using a physical act as punishment (i.e., you bit your brother so I will bite you). You can use the problem-solving model discussed in this chapter to help your child identify the source of problems that lead to aggressive behavior and explore alternatives for dealing with them. As numerous authors and researchers have observed, the combination of hyperactivity and serious aggression, left untreated, is a time bomb waiting to explode.

REMEMBER . . .

✦ Aggressive behavior is not a symptom of hyperactivity.

✦ The majority of hyperactive children experience either less popularity due to social skills weaknesses or rejection due to the exhibition of aggressive, inappropriate behavior.

✦ The ability to make and keep friends will help the hyperactive child in other areas, including behavior at home and at school.

✦ It has been suggested that the three most important skills hyperactive children must possess for social success are the ability to engage in rough play appropriately, the ability to make appropriate verbal requests, and the ability to compliment others.

✦ For many hyperactive children, social problems result from a combination of hyperactivity and other developmental impairments such as a language disability.

✦ Teaching a logical model to identify and solve problems is an essential component of the hyperactive child's treatment plan.

CHAPTER 6

The Hyperactive Child at School: Fitting a Round Peg into a Square Hole

Josh is an 8-year-old second grader. He has been a challenge to his teachers. Although Josh was the same size and appearance as the other children, he was frequently described by his kindergarten teacher as immature. Despite two years of preschool, Josh seemed unable to fit into the routine of kindergarten. He did not pay attention, he did not finish even simple tasks consistently, he was restless and fidgety in his seat, he was quite emotional and cried frequently, and he became overexcited easily and frequently drew attention to himself in a negative way. Although Josh was academically able, he frequently failed to finish his work and appeared to his teacher to be slower at grasping new academic ideas. With other children, Josh was impulsive and frequently behaved inappropriately, and so he was soon excluded from social activities. By second grade, this pattern had intensified. As the result of his frustration, Josh became the class clown. Because he continued to have difficulty remaining on task, he frequently sought reasons for not completing schoolwork. Josh continued to have problems with other children and in response to their rejection had been involved in a number of fights. He was also unable to participate actively in an appropriate way during group instruction. Josh was increasingly aware of his problems. His parents and teachers had exhausted themselves and their resources in an attempt to understand and help him succeed at school.

By school age, the hyperactive child begins to venture out into the world and no longer has the family to act as a buffer. Behavior that was once accepted as cute or immature is no longer tolerated. The hyperactive kindergartner must now learn to deal with the rules, structure, and limits of organized education, and his temperament simply does not fit well within the expectations of school. His behavior quickly takes up a disproportionately large percentage of the teacher's time. Unfortunately, this attention from the teacher is often negative and directed at the child for not doing what is expected. This further disrupts the classroom because there are many other children who would prefer watching the teacher and hyperactive child do battle rather than completing their own work.

Some researchers have suggested that hyperactive children are simply not as intelligent as other children. This idea, however, must be viewed cautiously. To succeed on tests, a child must not only demonstrate the skills being evaluated but possess the ability to listen to and follow instructions, pay attention, and persist until the test is completed. The child must also be able to stop and consider what the best possible answer might be from a number of choices. Hyperactive children, however, are weak in these skill areas and thus tests of intelligence may often provide better measures of their hyperactivity than of their intellectual potential. It is fair to say that hyperactive children exhibit a normal range of intellectual skills. Some hyperactive children are very bright. Most fall within the average range, and some unfortunately are below average in their intellectual skills.

Very bright hyperactive children often manage to perform successfully during elementary school and may not be seen as having problems. The child's higher intellectual skills allow him to compensate for his inability to remain on task. He may not work for very long but the time spent on tasks often results in complete, frequently correct work. This child may not seem to pay attention, but when called on usually knows the right answer. Remember, being inattentive is not the equivalent of being unable to learn. Hyperactive children, when their attention is focused, are capable of learning as well as other children. Often, a careful review of the bright, hyperactive child's report cards reveals teacher's comments throughout elementary school concerning the child's difficulty paying attention and sitting still.

In junior high school, however, even the most intelligent hyperactive adolescent cannot consistently keep up with the increased educational demands and responsibilities necessary for success. It is frequently during the junior high school years that intelligent hyperactive adolescents are recognized as experiencing this pattern of temperamental difficulty, which interferes with their school performance.

Some researchers have suggested that hyperactive children do not learn as well as other children at school, and many are so impaired in their ability to learn that they might be referred to as learning disabled. Some studies in the 1970s suggested that 40% to 80% of hyperactive children experience a specific learning disability (difficulty with reading, spelling, mathematics, written or spoken language). It was suggested that these children have difficulty completing tasks not just because of their inattention but because they are less capable of learning than other children.

More recent research studies have found that approximately 10% to 30% of hyperactive children exhibit delays in academic skills sufficient to warrant a diagnosis of learning disability. Sally and Bennett Shaywitz, physicians and researchers, have concluded that although the majority of hyperactive children do not experience learning disabilities, the percentage of learning-disabled children who are hyperactive constitute a significant group of the learning-disabled population. Starting with the population of learning-disabled children, it is estimated the approximately one third of this group also experience problems of hyperactivity.

Although the overlap between learning disability and hyperactivity is real, it is not fair to conclude that all or even the majority of hyperactive children are also learning disabled. Thus, the relationship between hyperactivity and learning disability is not clear and these are probably two separate disorders of childhood with the occurrence of one not necessarily predicting the occurrence of the other.

Hyperactive children may not perform well academically, but as a group most appear to have equal potential to learn as normal children. By the later school years, however, the long-term impact of not paying attention or completing work eventually has a negative effect on academic achievement. The lack of basic attention skills, as well as the lack of practice in utilizing those skills, begins to take a toll on achievement.

One of the most common observations made by elementary school teachers about hyperactive children is that they appear to be daydreaming. These children are not daydreaming but are interested in something other than what the teacher may be focusing on at the time. The hyperactive child usually is involved in more nonproductive activity during work and free time than the other children. The hyperactive child's behavior is uneven, unpredictable, and unresponsive to usual teacher interventions. The hyperactive child may complete a task one day but be unable to complete a similar task the next day. This often results in interpreting the child's behavior as noncompliant. That is, this child can do it but simply does not choose to do so. So the teacher increases the pressure. For the majority of hyperactive children, however, this is an incorrect interpretation, and because the child is not engaging purposefully in this behavior, attempts to force the issue are not successful. Increased frustration for both the teacher and child is the result.

Many hyperactive children also experience a wide range of secondary behavioral or emotional problems at school as the result of their inability to meet the demands of the classroom. These problems often develop in response to frequent and repeated failure. In response, some children become depressed and withdrawn, while others become angry and aggressive.

By first or second grade, other children become increasingly aware of the hyperactive child's classroom inabilities. Studies of children at school frequently conclude that the hyperactive child is not chosen by other children as a best friend, seatmate, or partner in activities. Research in which children with no prior knowledge of each other were placed together for short play periods resulted in the majority of hyperactive children being nominated by the other children as someone whom they did not want to play with again after the play period. When interviewed, hyperactive children are well aware of this rejection. Often, to protect a fragile self-image, they deny these problems or blame their difficulties on others.

The hyperactive child has a powerful effect on the teacher's behavior toward the class as a whole. Studies have shown that overall, negative interactions between teachers and all the children in the class were higher in classrooms with hyperactive children who had significant problems. Teachers of hyperactive children are often more directive and controlling in their interactions not only with these children but with other children in the classroom too. In addition, the rate of conflict between the other children in the classroom also appears to be higher when the hyperactive child is not being dealt with effectively.

As we discussed in Chapter 5, hyperactive children are often immature and incompetent when it comes to social skills. Frequently even their best efforts fail. Their social-skill deficiencies result in a pattern of high-incidence, low-impact behaviors. They may be incompetent in their ability to join an ongoing conversation, take turns, or cooperate. These are not terrible problems, but they result in the hyperactive child being less popular and not well accepted. Some hyperactive children also exhibit a pattern of low-incidence, high-impact behaviors. These behaviors are frequently aggressive. Although they may not occur more than once or twice per day, they very quickly result in the hyperactive child being rejected and disliked by others.

QUALITIES THAT HELP PARENTS COPE WITH SCHOOL PROBLEMS

It is not surprising that hyperactive children have experienced increasing problems at school over the past 20 years. Successful school performance has become increasingly dependent on a child's ability to concentrate for long periods of time, sit still, stay on task, and wait months to receive a report card as a reward for hundreds of hours of work. Our schools are demanding more and more from children at younger and younger ages. It is important for parents and teachers to understand the mechanics of our educational system and the reasons hyperactive children have a high probability of not being able to meet the demands of the classroom.

Problems at school are frequently the number one complaint by parents of hyperactive children to professionals. Although the child's behavior at home may be particularly aversive, it is at school that the child begins to learn about the world and must interact with many others. Parents often feel helpless and frustrated. They may be exposed year in and year out to repeated complaints and concerns from teachers, school psychologists, and special educators. The best efforts of school personnel may be unsuccessful. Even medicated hyperactive children continue to present some problems beyond the ordinary at school. Is there something parents can do to increase the chances that their hyperactive child will be successful at school? Can parents make a difference? Absolutely!

Parents of children must be *patient, persistent,* and *proud.* They must be willing to patiently educate teachers about attention disorders in childhood, and offer resources, understanding, and support. Parents of hyperactive children must be persistent in their efforts to help their child attain scholastic success. They must learn to negotiate and compromise, and to recognize what kinds of intervention are feasible for classroom teachers and special educators to administer. Parents must be willing to provide additional assistance in the form of suggestions for behavioral management programs that can be implemented at school and followed through at home. Classroom teachers are very receptive to such ideas, especially when they have exhausted their own repertoire.

Parents must also be willing to enlist the aide of a community psychologist or educator to work with the school team. Finally, parents must be proud. They must work to help teachers understand that there are assets and potential in every child. Parents must help teachers learn to seek out, nurture, and reinforce what is positive in the hyperactive child, and to understand that over time this child can and must be made a contributing member of the school community. Just as it is important for parents to put themselves in their child's position to help the child cope, it is equally important for the parent to see things from the teacher's perspective. Teachers must also be open and honest with parents. As one teacher has commented, parents must be included because "after all they know their child much better than you do and can offer valuable ideas."

It is also important to remember that just as our children are unique and different, so are teachers. They too are human beings. Therefore, no single set of guidelines and suggestions will work for every teacher and with every hyperactive child. It is a matter of comfort, personality, and fit. Often, many different interventions must be attempted before success is achieved.

FINDING THE RIGHT CLASSROOM

At this point you are probably well aware that a crucial factor in your child's success at school is his teacher and the teacher's ability to manage a classroom effectively. One set of parents sadly and somewhat confusedly related this story about their child's successes and failures at school.

Kindergarten went poorly, yet first grade went well. Second grade started out well, but slowly deteriorated. Third grade started out poorly, but by the end of the year their hyperactive son was nominated as the most improved student. In fourth grade things started out well then again slowly deteriorated. A careful review of the child's history and report cards suggested that in successful years this child's teachers had the ability to understand the child's temperamental difficulties and effectively intervene in a positive way. In the negative years, there was an initial carryover from the prior year's positive experience, but slowly the teacher's punitive, often negative reinforcement methods for managing problems of incompetence resulted in things getting worse instead of improving.

Whether your child is receiving special education services or not, we believe that you are entitled to participate actively in the selection of your child's teachers. The following is a checklist of what to look for in the ideal teacher and classroom environment for the hyperactive child. These suggestions are based on a combination of scientific research, professional judgment, and common sense. Some of these issues can be addressed by speaking directly with prospective teachers, others by speaking with parents whose children have worked with a particular teacher, while others can be evaluated by observing the classroom. This checklist can also serve as a guideline for designing a classroom for a hyperactive child.

_____ The teacher is knowledgeable about hyperactivity in childhood and willing to acknowledge that this problem has a significant impact on children in the classroom.

_____ The teacher appears to understand the difference between problems that result from incompetence and problems that result from noncompliance.

_____ The teacher does not primarily employ negative reinforcement or punishment as a means of managing problems and motivating children in the classroom.

_____ The classroom is organized.

_____ There are a clear and consistent set of class rules. All students are required to learn the rules.

_____ Classroom rules are clearly posted for all to see.

_____ There is a consistent and predictable schedule in the classroom.

_____ The teacher demands and follows through with specific requirements for behavior and productivity.

_____ Academic work is provided at children's ability level.

_____ The teacher is interested in process (understanding a concept) rather than product (completing 50 subtraction problems).

_____ The classroom arrangement is set up with separate desks arranged in rows.

_____ The teacher distributes small, consistent, frequent social and material rewards.

_____ The classroom teacher is able to use a modified response cost program (see Chapter 7) with the hyperactive child if needed.

_____ The teacher employs brief punishments accompanied by directions to return to work when the hyperactive child disrupts the work of others.

_____ The teacher ignores daydreaming or off-task behavior that does not disrupt others, and then uses differential attention (paying attention to the child) when the youngster returns to work.

_____ The smallest student-to-teacher ratio possible (preferably one teacher to 8 students; realistically no more than one teacher to 20 students).

_____ The teacher is willing to intersperse high- and low-interest activities throughout the day rather than having the student complete all work in the morning with one, repetitive task after another.

_____ The teacher is willing to provide additional supervision during transition times between classes, recess, and during other large activities such as assemblies.

_____ The teacher is able to anticipate problems and plan ahead to avoid those problems.

_____ The teacher is willing to assist the hyperactive child learn, practice, and maintain organizational skills.

_____ The teacher is willing to accept responsibility to see to it that the hyperactive child learns and effectively uses a system to keep track of homework and that he leaves the school building every day with that homework.

_____ The teacher accepts responsibility for ongoing communication with parents. A daily note is sent home for elementary students. A weekly progress note is used for junior and senior high school students.

_____ The teacher provides brief instructions, directly and at a level the hyperactive child can understand.

_____ The teacher is able to maintain effective control over the entire classroom as well as the hyperactive child. A visitor to such a classroom should be impressed by the organization and efficiency of the students.

_____ Preferably, this is a closed classroom (four walls and a door).

_____ The teacher is willing to develop a system so that directions are repeated and offered in a variety of ways.

_____ The teacher is willing to provide cues to help the hyperactive child return to task and avoid becoming overaroused.

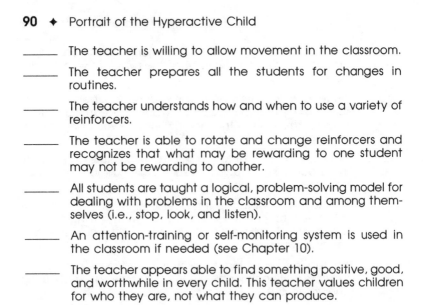

_____ The teacher is willing to allow movement in the classroom.

_____ The teacher prepares all the students for changes in routines.

_____ The teacher understands how and when to use a variety of reinforcers.

_____ The teacher is able to rotate and change reinforcers and recognizes that what may be rewarding to one student may not be rewarding to another.

_____ All students are taught a logical, problem-solving model for dealing with problems in the classroom and among themselves (i.e., stop, look, and listen).

_____ An attention-training or self-monitoring system is used in the classroom if needed (see Chapter 10).

_____ The teacher appears able to find something positive, good, and worthwhile in every child. This teacher values children for who they are, not what they can produce.

All these issues are important in classrooms for adolescents as well. Unfortunately, parents will not have as much opportunity to evaluate the many teachers adolescents encounter in a single semester. Nonetheless, it is important to try and get to know each teacher. Carefully evaluate your teen's performance in each class during the first few weeks. In some situations, go as far as to change teachers if a particular instructor is rigid and unwilling to compromise. A tutor, tracking class, and second set of textbooks left at home are also effective interventions for the hyperactive adolescent.

It has been our experience that while skills-building groups, lasting anywhere from four to eight weeks, may teach valuable skills, the hyperactive adolescent often does not use those skills without consistent, ongoing support. It is recommended that even hyperactive adolescents who are academically advanced participate in weekly academic therapy to learn executive skills such as planning, organization, and problem solving. In some school systems, it is also possible for hyperactive adolescents to participate in a daily tracking class without being classified in the special education system. During one period a day (usually the last) the hyperactive adolescent works in a small group setting with a teacher whose principal job it is to help the adolescent to review what has taken place in each class that day, to know what homework is required, and to prepare to take home all materials necessary to complete homework. In some school systems, however, a tracking class may not be available unless the student is placed in the special education system. Changes in special education law in many states are now allowing hyperactive adolescents who do not experience specific learning or behavioral problems to receive special education services.

HELPING WITH HOMEWORK

Homework is probably the most stressful activity parents and their hyperactive children engage in. Children are tired after school and wish to play. Research has also suggested that normal daily fatigue has a negative impact on the hyperactive child's skills. Parents feel pressured to meet the school's demands. Often, hyperactive children bring home work that was not completed during the regular school day. With elementary school students, parents must spend time working directly with their child, preferably right after school. With adolescents, it is suggested that a specific time be set aside for homework each day and that parents work gradually toward helping the adolescent complete homework independently. The following list is a summary of suggestions, by author Mary Landers (Helping the LD Child with Homework. Academic Therapy Journal, Nov. 1984), to help children and parents with homework. Where appropriate, the suggestions have been modified to better suit the needs of hyperactive children.

1. If your child does not want your help with homework, forcing the issue will only result in more conflict and less motivation. Provide incentives, offer assistance, but do not insist that your child allow you to help with homework.

2. Establish a routine and set goals. Consistency is an important part of learning. Designate a specific area for homework and a fixed study time. Try to divide homework into tasks that can be completed independently and tasks that must be worked on as a team between you and your child.

3. Agree on who will assist with homework. One parent or another may work better with a particular child. It is important for parents to be patient, fair, flexible, and consistent. Parents must instill confidence, demonstrate a positive attitude, and listen carefully to what the child has to say. It is also important for parents to be sensitive to the child's feelings and frustration level.

4. Parents must give clear directions, ask for the child's opinion, and gain the child's trust.

5. Homework sessions must be successful. Begin homework by having the child complete the easiest problems first to establish success and reinforcement.

6. Keep your comments task oriented. Emphasize the task at hand, not your values. The solution to a problem may be apparent to you but not to your child. Do not digress to nonproductive comments in such situations. Your comments should give the child direction for accomplishing the task based on the child's skills. Making comments related to your anger or fears about the child's future or effort only heightens anxiety and will not lead to greater productivity.

7. It is important to accept all the child's responses as genuine. If a homework routine is not working, try altering it rather than disciplining your child.

8. Don't allow weaknesses in reading to interfere with activities in related subjects such as history or science. A history or science homework assignment can quickly become a remedial reading lesson. This is nonproductive. This approach will not only lead to a dislike for reading but for other subjects as well.

9. Avoid excessive corrections. Look for similarities in mistakes and point them out. Excessive correction stands the risk of leading to greater feelings or poor self-worth and incompetence.

10. Be honest but sensitive when providing feedback. Seek out the best in your child and reinforce it. Praise your child for his effort.

11. Don't be afraid to speak up on your child's behalf, if you believe there is too much or excessively repetitive homework. Hyperactive children will not perform well at repetitive, rote assignments. If this is the majority of what comes home, some changes are needed.

12. Plan shorter homework times. Remember, hyperactive children do not persist well and may become easily bored with repetitive activities. Homework time should not be late in the day when the child is tired and may be experiencing rebound irritability as medication wears off. A number of shorter homework periods interspersed with reinforcement time earlier in the afternoon is preferable.

SHOULD ALL HYPERACTIVE CHILDREN BE IN SPECIAL CLASSES?

No! With the combination of appropriate medical and non-medical intervention, the majority of children who are just hyperactive can and must be successfully educated in regular classroom settings. It is important for parents to remember, however, that approximately 10% to 30% of hyperactive children also experience a specific learning disability and must receive some form of special education. Approximately another 30% experience disruptive behavior problems that may require work with the school psychologist, in a group or on an individual basis. Some of these children may also need to be placed in a special education classroom for part of their day to complete their work so as not to disrupt others. In addition, a very small percentage may require placement in special classes for most of the day.

In all likelihood, there will be an increase in programs for hyperactive children as federal and state legislation mandates schools to identify and to provide services. While a number of specialized private programs for hyperactive students exist across the country, most communities do not have such resources. Nor do most hyperactive students require this type of placement.

REMEMBER . . .

✦ Some hyperactive children experience difficulty learning academic tasks; most, however, are able to learn and often do so even though they do not pay attention consistently or complete work effectively.

✦ Teachers of hyperactive children are often as frustrated as parents.

✦ Success in school for the hyperactive child requires a combination of medical, cognitive, and management interventions.

✦ With assistance, most hyperactive children can succeed in the regular classroom.

CHAPTER 7

The Hyperactive Child at Home: The Scapegoat

We had occasion to work with 9-year-old Jimmy, a typical, hyperactive child struggling at home, with friends, and at school. Slowly, a combination of medical and nonmedical treatments began to make a positive difference in Jimmy's life. Unfortunately, Jimmy's 13-year-old sister and 8-year-old brother had an emotional investment in Jimmy's continuing to have problems. Although both Jimmy's siblings disliked his behavior and its impact on their lives, they found a convenient way of dealing with this problem: they made Jimmy the family scapegoat. Whenever anything went wrong, Jimmy was immediately blamed, often for a sibling's behavior. And since problems were often Jimmy's fault anyway, Jimmy's parents usually accepted the sibling's explanation. The siblings were very creative, and despite our efforts toward improvement at home, Jimmy continued to struggle. We decided to have the older sister and younger brother visit us in the hope that we could help them understand Jimmy's problems and end this destructive pattern of behavior. The two siblings arrived with a list of reasons the family would be better off if Jimmy went to live in a foster home. They were very convincing. They were also very powerful. Jimmy was a convenient scapegoat and they were not about to give him up. They wanted to have their cake and eat it too. They complained about Jimmy, yet not quite so loudly that sufficient action would be taken to ensure that he no longer would be the scapegoat.

The significant, and at times unexpected, impact the hyperactive child has on family members and the community cannot be underestimated. As author and psychologist Dr. John Taylor (*Helping Your Hyperactive Child,* Prima Publishers, 1990) has noted, hyperactive children can "emotionally bankrupt" a family. Because of the hyperactive child's inability to conform to parent, sibling, and community expectations of appropriate behavior, the child forms a very different parent–child bond and engages in frequent conflicts with siblings. Research by Dr. Russell Barkley has suggested that families of hyperactive children undergo more divorces and more geographic moves. Whether these factors are contributed to by the hyperactive child's difficulties or worsen the hyperactive child's problems is unclear. Nonetheless, it is well accepted that families of hyperactive children have a higher risk for all kinds of problems. As author Dr. L. Eugene Arnold (*Helping Parents Help Their Children,* Brunner-Mazel, 1978) has observed, the chronic nature of the hyperactive child's problems not only represent a financial and emotional drain on the family but also drain the family of time, energy, relationships, and mental health.

Mothers and fathers of hyperactive children frequently disagree concerning parenting techniques and strategies. Mothers are often left to bear the pressure of day-to-day interaction with the hyperactive child. They must prepare the child for school in the morning, receive the child after school, attempt to handle duties of the home while managing the child, and deal with homework, friends, and bedtime routine. Fathers, on the other hand, often have many fewer interactions with the hyperactive child. When they do interact, they often spend time in enjoyable rather than routine activities. It is not surprising, therefore, that mothers frequently have more complaints than fathers. Nor is it surprising that mothers are often perceived by their spouses as the source of the child's problems. "You're not tough enough" or "You let him get away with too much" echoes in the homes of many hyperactive children. Generally, when fathers attempt to play more of a caretaker role, they too very quickly become aware of the child's difficulties.

It is also not uncommon for hyperactive children to respond more consistently to their fathers than their mothers. This is probably a cultural phenomenon. In our society, men are seen as more powerful, dominant, and controlling. Fathers are more likely to use punitive force with their children than mothers. Fathers are also less likely to engage in repeated verbal banter to get the hyperactive child to accomplish a task. Mothers are more likely to use affection to manage behavior problems. For these and probably other reasons, the hyperactive child may respond more quickly to fathers than to mothers.

Brothers and sisters of the hyperactive child very quickly become aware that this child garners more negative attention from parents than anyone else. Their reactions can be varied. Some react with anger and frustration because this child is excused from activities and responsibilities or has more opportunity to earn rewards for behavior that is routinely expected from them without reward. As with Jimmy, the hyperactive child's problems become a double-edged sword with siblings. Brothers and sisters may be jealous and angry on the one hand, yet have a vested interest in maintaining the hyperactive child in his role. So, the hyperactive child, as in Jimmy's case, becomes a convenient scapegoat. He can take the blame for everything from a plate being broken to a visit to an amusement park being cut short. Of greater concern though is the potential long term, negative impact hyperactivity can have on sibling relationships.

Avoidance becomes a parent's main strategy. After repeated unsuccessful attempts at shopping, church, scouting, even everyday neighborhood activities, many parents choose isolation and segregation as a means of avoiding further problems. Although in the short run this may be an effective intervention, in the long run it further isolates the family from needed community support, affects the hyperactive child's siblings, and probably does not make much of a positive difference.

It is fair to say that the hyperactive child becomes the family problem. In families with more than one hyperactive child, the impact is even greater. In families in which the parents' and child's temperaments do not mesh, problems may intensify. Parents repeated unsuccessful attempts at disciplining the hyperactive child have a significant impact on their relationship. Often, many parents are so burnt out by the daily demands of caring for their hyperactive child that little if any time is left for enjoyment or pleasure. The child is seen as a burden and an unfair responsibility. Parents become angry, frustrated, and often intolerant.

As with any problem, certain information and ideas obtained by parents are erroneous and can lead to the escalation, rather than the solution of problems. As they begin to recognize that their hyperactive child is different, parents tend to formulate one of two ideas. Either they perceive themselves as normal and this child as bad or damaged, or they perceive the child as normal and themselves as poor or inadequate parents. Either extreme can be equally damaging and hinder the effective management of your hyperactive child. The first leads to anger and resentment. The second leads to guilt and possibly overpermissiveness.

From these two ideas, parents form a variety of misconceptions about their hyperactive child, fueled by everything they read and hear, ranging from information in the *Reader's Digest* to the *National Enquirer.* Common problems often lead to a variety of common, frequently inaccurate beliefs. Hyperactivity as a childhood problem is no different. Some of these misconceptions are probably already familiar to you.

MISCONCEPTIONS

Wait, He'll Outgrow It

The comment that most frequently results from this misconception is "he is just a boy." Since he is just a boy, therefore, parents are expected to excuse or overlook inattention, hyperactivity, and impulsiveness. The implication is that the child is normal and parents are wrong and intolerant. Unfortunately, the majority of children grow into their hyperactivity not out of it.

Bad Mothering

This misconception also has its roots in the normal child–bad parent fallacy. As we have noted, it is frequently fostered by fathers. The second most frequent culprits are grandparents. Mothers are perceived as being either too permissive, overly demanding, or generally not tough enough. The child is seen as normal but requiring more consistent discipline. This misconception is often fueled when the child, during brief visits with grandparents, is entertained and behaves well, or when the child behaves well during one of his father's infrequent interactions during routine activities.

Guilt

This often goes hand in hand with the idea that the mother is at fault. Usually it enters the picture after mothers have been repeatedly counseled by others that they are inadequate parents. This leads to self-blame, self-doubt, feelings of inadequacy, and second guessing. One parent reported to the authors that she was told by a mental health counselor that the reason her child was unable to pay attention and complete schoolwork was because she "pushed him too hard" during toilet training. The acceptance of guilt on the mother's part leads to depression, angry resentment, or over-permissiveness. All three do little, if anything, to improve family functioning and help the hyperactive child.

He Just Doesn't Want to Listen

This the most benign and seductive of the misconceptions. It assumes the child is inattentive, hyperactive, and impulsive on purpose. It often results from the hyperactive child's inconsistency. Because the child can pay attention when sufficiently motivated or sit still when an enticing reward is offered, parents conclude that the child must be bribed to pay attention or behave. It leads parents to assume that most of the child's problems result from noncompliance rather than incompetence. It leads to increasingly punitive, negative, and punishing interventions. The increasing failure of these interventions usually creates additional family stress and leads to a variety of secondary behavior and mood problems in the hyperactive child.

The Bad Seed

This is the "he's doing it on purpose" misconception taken to extreme. As with the play of a similar name by Maxwell Anderson, the assumption is that this child is evil: that his actions are planned, premeditated, and designed to serve his benefits at the expense of everyone else. This is a dead end notion that very quickly bankrupts the family emotionally. Punishing solutions are ineffective and resentment on the parents' part grows like a cancer.

It's Everyone Else's Fault

Some parents, possibly because of their own feelings of guilt, arrive at the conclusion that the hyperactive child's problems stem from the manner in which the child is treated by siblings, friends, relatives, and teachers. Parents who embrace this idea very quickly become overinvolved in defending the child. Although hyperactive children certainly need support from their parents, the overinvolvement that results from blaming others interferes with parents' ability realistically to understand the child's actual impact on his surroundings. Thus, it postpones the taking of appropriate action.

Bad Karma

Parents who foster this misconception are influenced unfortunately by erroneous information concerning the origin of appropriate methods of helping hyperactive children. Although we have not worked with a parent who believed their child's problems stemmed from bad karma or from the alignment of the moon and stars, we have had the opportunity to work with parents who believed their child's primary hyperactive problems stemmed from poor diet, inadequate vitamins, fluorescent lights, cultural pressures, or middle ear imbalance. Out of desperation, parents embrace one or more of these fringe explanations to cure hyperactivity. They invest large amounts of energy and money to pursue treatments that are no more effective than luck.

WHAT PARENTS MUST DO

Education

The importance of education cannot be overemphasized. To effectively manage an incurable problem such as hyperactivity, appropriate education is essential. Education is important because a parent not only must know how to proceed but how to interpret both wanted and unsolicited information about the child's problems and its solutions. In one way or another, your hyperactive child will continue to experience more problems throughout his childhood and teenage years than the majority of other children. You must be aware of resources that are helpful in identifying problems and strategies for effective coping because your hyperactive child will need your help to succeed.

You must believe that with your help, appropriate community support, and intervention, your hyperactive child can and will succeed. It is important to start a resource library. No single book, video, or audio cassette is going to address all your needs and provide all the information necessary, but you must become an educated consumer. All the resources listed in the Appendix provide helpful suggestions. However, hyperactive children are not identical. Parents are different too. You must learn how to use these resources and take from them only the information that will be useful to you.

It is also important for you to join a parent support group. Parents supporting other parents is an essential component of any effective management program.

Control

To effectively manage your hyperactive child's problems, you must be in control. Your patience, skill, tolerance, knowledge, understanding and, most of all, ability to recognize and acknowledge the love you have for your hyperactive child are essential in diffusing daily problems. Your ability to stay in control will minimize the chances that your child will develop secondary emotional problems, such as depression or more serious conduct problems.

Find Ways to Enjoy Your Child

Parents of hyperactive children often become so caught up in management that they neglect important opportunities for enjoyment. It is important to spend some time each day engaged in an enjoyable activity. As one parent commented to us, "We are going to spend some enjoyable time together each day, even if it kills us!" Dr. L. Eugene Arnold has noted that some children must be "force-fed affection." Seek out and find positive attributes in your hyperactive child. Acknowledge them; nurture them; and help them develop.

Parental Support

It is important for spouses to support each other. All too often we see only mothers during assessment and treatment. In many cases we are informed that father acknowledges a problem but chooses to not participate. In other situations, the father disagrees with the nature of the child's problems, fosters one of the many misconceptions, and in fact becomes a significant hurdle in improving the life of his hyperactive child. Unless parents can work together, it is virtually impossible to bring about positive change at home. Often we spend as much time helping parents identify, define, and agree on problems and interventions as we do implementing them. But this time is essential if interventions are to be successful overall and especially if they are to minimize the hyperactive child's impact on what might be an already stressful and tenuous marital relationship.

School

As we have already discussed, parents must be open about their child's problems and tolerant of the teacher's position. They must be willing to help teachers understand their child's history and patient when teachers express frustration concerning the child's school problems. Success at school is essential for your hyperactive child.

Build Self-Esteem

Hyperactive children do not experience as many positive interactions with adults, friends, and teachers as other children. They do not succeed as often or as well as other children in athletics, scouting, or chores. For these reasons, it is most important that you help your hyperactive child develop his talents. Determine what he is good at doing, nurture it, and develop it, whether it is dance, athletics, or stamp collecting. Your child must be able to find something in his life that he can accomplish and feel good about.

Friends

Parents of hyperactive children, as we discussed in Chapter 5, must understand the social problems their child is likely to experience and be willing to take the time necessary to help the child initiate and maintain friendships. Success with friends is an important factor, predicting more positive adolescent and, probably, adult outcome for hyperactive children.

Siblings

Don't forget the other children in the family. Your hyperactive child will require time, management, and adjustment of routine and schedules to function effectively. He will demand an inordinately greater amount of your time than you may be able to offer to your other children. It is important to recognize and acknowledge this phenomenon as well as to be honest with your other children concerning the hyperactive sibling's needs. You can attempt to compensate for this difference by providing additional rewards, activities, and praise, for siblings and their accomplishments. Remember, all your children need your time and involvement.

REMEMBER . . .

✦ Untreated hyperactive children can emotionally bankrupt a family.

✦ Hyperactive children usually respond better to fathers than mothers.

✦ Brothers and sisters of hyperactive children may form a love–hate relationship, disliking the extra attention the hyperactive child garners, yet using the child's mistakes and failures as a means of making themselves look better.

✦ Avoidance is not an effective long-term intervention for hyperactive children.

✦ Parents frequently form two sets of misconceptions, either assuming the child is normal and they are not, or vice versa. Watch out for these.

✦ Parent education, control, enjoyment, family unity, good friends, and school success are essential components in the formula for success for the hyperactive child.

CHAPTER 8

The Hyperactive
Teenager and Adult:
Who Will Succeed and
Who Will Fail?

On his sixteenth birthday, Brian decided that it was time for him to drive, despite having not yet passed drivers' education or taken his final license examination. Brian borrowed the family car and rear-ended another vehicle, which resulted in a multiple car accident. Fortunately, no one was hurt. But this was not Brian's first impulsive teenage act. Despite attempts by teachers, parents, and his physician to provide both medical and nonmedical treatments for his hyperactivity when he was younger, Brian continued to exhibit a pattern of inattentive, impulsive, and hyperactive problems as a teenager. His behavior frequently alienated friends and relatives, and he often found himself alone or with other adolescents experiencing similar adjustment problems. He had been caught shoplifting twice, once in possession of alcohol, and once joyriding in a car another teenager had borrowed. Brian's parents were angry and frustrated.

They were tired of the years of coping and attempting to accept Brian's hyperactive problems. His parents and teachers, however, did not realize that for quite some time Brian had been feeling increasingly rejected and pessimistic about his life. He had had suicidal thoughts, and after this automobile accident finally decided to seek counseling because he was seriously considering suicide.

Stuart, on the other hand, had a similar history of hyperactivity. However, he did not experience the social and problems with authority that plagued Brian. As he entered adolescence, although Stuart continued to struggle academically, he managed to maintain a network of friends and found success playing in the school orchestra. Although he continued to be inattentive and at times impulsive, he followed rules and limits, slowly gained greater acceptance by friends and teachers, and seemed generally satisfied with the course of his life.

THE HYPERACTIVE TEENAGER

Professionals once counseled parents that hyperactivity was a disorder that affected only young children. Problems of hyperactivity, professionals insisted, were for the most part outgrown by the teenage years. Eventually, we have gathered sufficient data to suggest that some of the primary symptoms of hyperactivity may diminish in their intensity as children reach adolescence, but hyperactivity continues to plague and cause problems for many teenagers.

In research studies, 20% to 60% of hyperactive teenagers are involved in antisocial behavior that results in referral to juvenile court. It is estimated that approximately 3% to 4% of the normal population of teenagers ends up in juvenile court. In other studies, 35% of hyperactive teenagers were suspended from school at least once as opposed to only 8% to 10% of the normal population. Finally, by high school, it is estimated that as many as 80% of hyperactive teenagers are behind at least one year in at least one basic academic subject. It appears that the secondary problems of hyperactivity involving school performance, social relations, and the ability to follow society's rules and limits, persist, intensify, and become more complex for the hyperactive teenager.

In his recent text, *The Troubled Adolescent,* (Pergamon Press, 1990) Dr. Joseph White describes the five mixed messages that confront teenagers and influence important decisions concerning their values and behavior. In our fast-paced society, we address children as if they were adults and expect them to behave that way at ever younger ages. Young teens today must make decisions about expressing their sexual desires; working hard, and preparing for the future over seeking instant gratification; working for self alone or learning to cooperate and live harmoniously with others; following the rules or shaping the rules to suit their immediate needs; and using drugs and alcohol versus saying no. Even preteens confront some of these decisions. Children are maturing physically at earlier ages, and we expect younger children to make long-term commitments. Due to the increasing technical demands of our society, many young people attend college and maintain their dependence long into their 20s.

At one time, professionals suggested that the teenage years represented a terrible period of turmoil. Teenagers at risk due to other emotional, learning, or behavioral problems were assumed to be at even greater risk for serious teenage problems. Presumably, given the increased pressures of our society today, this phenomenon would have intensified. However, we are now aware that the teen years do not necessarily represent a trial by fire. Successful passage through the teenage years appears to be based on the teenager's ability to succeed in some area of his life. This usually involves success academically, socially, or in an extracurricular activity such as athletics, music, or dance. Hyperactive children, unfortunately, have histories of failure in these areas. Even the athletic, hyperactive teenager may have difficulty remaining on a team, not for lack of ability, but because of an inability to show up on time for practice and follow the coach's instructions.

It has also been suggested that many hyperactive teenagers have symptoms of depression as a result of their repeated failures and difficulties with friends. One study found that 25% of teenagers diagnosed with depression had histories of hyperactivity. Current research has affirmed that one out of four hyperactives will experience a depressive episode in childhood or adolescence. It is not surprising that hyperactive teenagers have been reported as lacking confidence and feeling helpless.

There is a high probability that hyperactive teenagers will not follow societies rules and limits well. Many find themselves involved with the law. When you are 7 and impulsively take another child's toy, you may get your hands slapped. However, when you are 17 and impulsively take someone's car, you end up in juvenile court. A recent study of 2,000 delinquents in the juvenile court system whose average age was 14, found that almost 50% had histories consistent with hyperactivity.

One of parents' greatest worries about the future stem from the statistics suggesting that a large percentage of hyperactive children progress to delinquency problems during their teenage years. In fact, parents of hyperactive teenagers are often more concerned about poor schoolwork, social difficulty, delinquency, and low self-esteem than with primary hyperactive symptoms such as inattention and restlessness. Recent long-term studies by Dr. Russell Barkley and others have addressed this issue as to which hyperactive children have the highest probability of experiencing teenage problems.

The studies suggest that hyperactivity alone only slightly increases the risk of delinquency and academic problems in the teenage years in comparison with the normal population. However, hyperactive children who also experience significant disruptive conduct problems from early childhood (see Chapter 9) have a greater chance of dropping out of school, experiencing problems with authority, and eventually ending up in the juvenile courts. These studies have begun to clarify the problem of what happens to hyperactive children when they become teenagers. It appears at this time that a child experiencing hyperactivity as well as another disruptive behavior disorder such as conduct or significant opposition, has a high probability of experiencing academic, social, or authority problems as a teenager.

Studies by Drs. Gabriel Weiss and Lillian Hechtman have suggested that hyperactive teenagers have a slightly higher incidence of automobile accidents than normal teens. It is also of interest that in this series of studies, five of the hyperactive teens who did not have licenses, also had automobile accidents while driving, yet none of the normal teens had accidents. A number of studies have also found that there is no greater probability of tobacco, alcohol, or drug abuse in hyperactive teens. However, if they also have some conduct problem they appear much more likely to abuse these substances.

Parents often ask about the length of time various medical and nonmedical treatments will be needed. Based on our current knowledge of hyperactivity, it is safe to say these treatments are needed throughout the adolescent years. Studies have suggested that approximately 80% of hyperactive teenagers have a history of receiving medication for at least three to five years. More than half have been involved in some form of counseling and psychotherapy for at least one to two years, while as many as 75% have received some form of special education for at least four to six years. Interestingly, in Dr. Barkley's long-term study, almost 50% of the mothers of hyperactive teenagers received psychotherapy in comparison with only 28% of the mothers of normal teens. In addition, 30% of the parents of hyperactive children had been involved in marital therapy compared with only 20% for the normal children.

Hyperactive teenagers with histories of minimal or unsuccessful treatment present a significant challenge for parents and professionals. These teenagers have a well-developed pattern of dealing with the world and they foster certain expectations about their ability to succeed using that approach. They are often resistant to help even when the solution, from our perspective, appears obvious. Hyperactive teenagers with histories of treatment failure are often unwilling to accept responsibility for their problems and are resistant to further treatment. Medical and nonmedical treatment must be set aside until the hyperactive teenager can be convinced to be an active rather than a passive participant. For many, the normal turbulence of family relations in adolescence is magnified, and the hyperactive teenager frequently finds his family both a source and focus of conflict. Family members become increasingly intolerant of the hyperactive teenager's impulsive and seemingly thoughtless style. This fuels further conflict.

Understanding Normal Adolescence and Hyperactivity

In their text, *Negotiating Parent–Adolescent Conflict,* (Guilford Press, 1989) Drs. Arthur Robin and Sharon Foster describe three major dimensions of family relations that determine how much conflict a family is likely to experience. The first dimension relates to difficulties in problem solving and communicating. Some family members have a difficult time sitting down, identifying problems, and communicating effectively so that they can implement successful solutions. The second dimension involves the formation of unreasonable ideas concerning family relations. A father may wrongly believe that if he allows his daughter to stay out after 10 P.M., she will run away and become pregnant. A son may believe that his parents *should always be fair* and allow him to do what he wants. Finally, the third dimension concerns disruption of normal structure where children are in charge or parental control is divided by one child or teen attempting to play one parent against the other.

These dimensions of family relations; weak communication skills, unreasonable ideas, and problems with family structure can exacerbate temperamental problems such as restlessness, inattention, and impulsiveness. Parents of hyperactive teenagers experience even greater difficulty during these years differentiating between problems of incompetence and those of noncompliance. As Drs. Robin and Foster point out, inattention results in the hyperactive adolescent being unable to remain on task when trying to resolve conflicts during family discussions, carry through with agreements, complete chores or homework, and meet parental expectations. The inability to tolerate frustration and the problems of overarousal some hyperactive teenagers experience lead to further arguments and confrontations. Impulsiveness may be misinterpreted as disrespect, and disorganization mislabeled as lack of effort and care.

What Does This Mean for You?

If you have a hyperactive teenager, all the issues discussed in Chapters 7 and 10 are important. Work together as a family with a professional to build problem-solving and communication skills between family members. It is important for you to stay in charge and avoid conflicts that may result from a lack of understanding.

THE HYPERACTIVE ADULT

John and Mike are both 28 years old. They have similar histories of childhood hyperactivity. They both struggled at school, had some difficulty with friends, and could not seem to please their parents at home. Yet as adults, they are very different. John attended college and although it took some time to learn effective study skills, he managed to graduate and enter the business world. At 28, his high energy level, willingness to take calculated risks, and ability to work long days and nights have resulted in a number of promotions and made him a valued member of his firm and the business community. Michael, unfortunately, dropped out of college, and at 28 has proceeded through a series of menial jobs. His lack of ability to follow through consistently at work and seeming disinterest in responsible activities have resulted in an unsatisfying career. He has been arrested a number of times for driving while intoxicated and has bounced a number of checks because he does not balance his checkbook. Michael and John both continue to exhibit symptoms consistent with their childhood hyperactivity, yet one has been able to turn what were once liabilities into assets. The other has not.

The toughest question we are asked by parents is not *what is wrong with my child* but *what will happen to my child when he grows up*. The earliest research dealing with hyperactive adults evaluated adults from various walks of life in an effort to identify whether childhood hyperactivity may have had some impact on their adult life. In these studies diagnosis of childhood hyperactivity was primarily based on reports of the adults and their memories of childhood. These initial studies were quite negative and most disturbing. They suggested that the majority of individuals experiencing significant life problems, such as those incarcerated for criminal activity, appeared to have histories of childhood hyperactivity. However, these studies had many serious flaws, the greatest of which was the inability to evaluate accurately what these individuals were really like when younger and the forces that affected them as children.

Over the past 10 years, recent studies have suggested that a variety of emotional problems may plague at least 50% of adults who were hyperactive children. Studies that have followed hyperactive children as they grew up have consistently found that this population in fact experiences emotional, academic, antisocial, and employment problems. Adults with histories of hyperactivity also appear to experience problems with anxiety, depression, and relationships. Unfortunately, the number of adults with histories of hyperactivity experiencing these problems is much greater than in the normal population. Also, in the long-term studies of Drs. Gabrielle Weiss and Lillian Hechtman, a considerably greater number of adults with histories of hyperactivity attempted suicide (10%) or died as a result of either suicide or accidental injury (5%) than those in the control groups.

In some long-term studies, a higher percentage of hyperactive children do not appear to complete high school or attend college in comparison with the normal population. They have a greater likelihood of having contact with the police and courts, usually for traffic violations. While the majority of adults with histories of hyperactivity do not demonstrate antisocial behavior, studies have suggested that perhaps as high as 25% continue to display persistent problems with conduct and substance abuse into adulthood. These problems are also present in the workplace. Although adults with histories of hyperactivity are usually employed and financially independent, the quality of their work and their upward vocational mobility falls short of the normal population.

Certainly all this information is quite depressing and emphasizes the increased risk hyperactive children have as they enter adulthood. Some professionals and authors choose to gloss over or minimize the importance of these data while focusing only on the majority of hyperactive children (probably as high as 50 to 70%) who manage to blend into society. This accomplishment, however, does not mean that they are doing as well or have progressed vocationally, emotionally, or academically as far as they had the potential to do. It simply means they are generally indistinguishable from others in the population.

The adult outcome data serve as a sobering kick in the backside, as it were, to help you understand the importance of early identification and long-term management. Research studies that have followed hyperactive children over many years suggest those children receiving medical, educational, and behavioral treatments over the long term show better adjustment and behavior than children receiving no treatment or just one treatment. A multidisciplinary treatment program for hyperactivity provides help to the child and family not only at home, in school, and with friends but also for psychological problems. Although research has suggested that as many as two thirds of hyperactive children outgrow their core symptoms, this does not mean that their personalities have not been affected. Nor does it mean that they will do as well in the world as might have been predicted by their intelligence or family history. Years of hyperactivity can take its toll on any child's adult outcome.

NONMEDICAL FACTORS THAT AFFECT OUTCOME

For years, the professional community has attempted to identify a specific treatment that might make a significant difference in what happens to hyperactive children and the kinds of adults they become. Unfortunately, we have not found that any one treatment, whether medical or nonmedical, makes a significant difference in predicting adult outcome. For example, it has not been found that children receiving medication for hyperactivity, function significantly better as adults than children who did not receive such medication. There are, however, a number of nontreatment or social factors that seem to hold out a better outcome in adulthood for hyperactive children.

Intelligence

Individuals who are more intelligent seem to make a better emotional adjustment in adult life and in the workplace. Hyperactive children with higher intelligence appear to fare better overall than their counterparts with average or below average intelligence.

Family Financial Status

Researchers have found that low-income families appear to have a higher incidence of poor medical and nutritional care for their children, tend to be less educated concerning appropriate child-rearing practices, and are more likely to experience psychological problems. High-income parents are more likely to seek and follow through with treatment. In addition, children from high-income families tend to grow up and reach status similar to or better than their parents.

Since a percentage of hyperactive children have parents with very similar problems, many of those families fall to the low-income strata, thereby providing further negative impact on the adult lives of their children. Some researchers have found that low-income families tend to have two to three times the number of children with hyperactivity symptoms as do high-income families.

Does this mean that children of low-income families are doomed to hyperactivity? Absolutely not! It is simply a factor that has been found to relate to hyperactivity and a poor adult outcome.

Friends

In general the best single predictor of appropriate emotional adjustment in adulthood is the ability to develop and maintain social contacts and friendships in childhood. Since hyperactive children have difficulty here, they are at greater risk for emotional problems in adulthood. Hyperactive children who have been successful at this endeavor usually adapt better to their hyperactivity and to the daily frustrations of home and school. In the long run, this success portends better adjusted adults.

Activity Level

Some studies have shown that the more active a child is in school, the greater the child's academic and achievement problems in later grades. It may be that activity level is a general marker of problem severity. More pronounced hyperactivity would be expected to result in lower achievement and performance as the demands of school increase.

Ability to Delay Rewards

Young children who are better than their peers at delaying rewards tend to develop into teenagers and young adults who can perform better on tests. They have greater success resisting negative temptation, demonstrate more appropriate social skills, and strive toward higher achievement.

Children who can delay rewards are also reported to be less aggressive than children who can't. Since difficulty delaying rewards is a hallmark of hyperactivity, it would not be surprising for this child to continue to experience problems into the teenage and adult years.

Aggression

Problems with aggression are not considered part of the hyperactivity syndrome. Aggression, however, is frequently present with hyperactivity. This behavior in childhood is also very closely related to parenting and family financial status. Families with low incomes appear to have more aggressive children.

Aggressive behavior is not always present in a hyperactive child. It has been found that 30% to 40% experience problems with aggression toward objects or people. This also occurs more frequently in the more restless, overactive child.

One of the best single predictors of conduct problems and poor emotional adjustment in the teenage years is a history of aggressive behavior in younger childhood. It appears that once a child develops this pattern, it is extremely difficult to change. As a society, we deal with aggressive behavior in kind; so it is not surprising that as we try to teach aggressive children to act differently, we may be reinforcing their behavior (i.e., you hit your brother, so I will hit you).

It is important for you to recognize aggressive or impaired conduct in your hyperactive child. This child is at much greater risk for problems in later life than he would be if he were simply hyperactive. It is also necessary to understand that the medical and nonmedical treatments traditionally used for hyperactivity are not usually effective over the long term, for reducing aggressive behavior.

Family Status and Mental Health

Unfortunately, some hyperactive children are born into families in which parents and other family members experience serious psychiatric problems. This makes it difficult, but not impossible, for professionals to treat the hyperactive child effectively. Although these parents may be unhappy with their hyperactive child, they frequently lack skills, persistence, and the ability to follow through with a treatment program.

Researchers have found that a history of psychiatric problems in parents increases the chances the hyperactive child will grow up and exhibit similar or related problems. In addition, parents of delinquents have been found to be less educated, make less use of available health services, and demonstrate less ability to obtain and hold a job than parents of nondelinquents. This suggests that overall this group of parents may not be as well adjusted or cope as well as other parents. Therefore, a hyperactive child or adolescent in such a family has a greater likelihood of having adult problems.

Parenting Style

Parents do not cause hyperactivity, but, the manner in which they interact with their children may increase or decrease the severity of hyperactive problems. Some studies have found that mothers who are more critical and directive are likely to worsen their child's problems.

These factors, however, have not been proven to cause hyperactivity. Nor do they perfectly predict whether or not a particular child will outgrow hyperactive symptoms. But these factors have been shown to be related to hyperactivity. Where they coexist they may predict which children with hyperactivity are most likely to succeed as adults. It is best to say that the adult outcome for a hyperactive child is related to a number of temperamental, intellectual, emotional, behavioral, therapeutic, family, and parenting factors. Some of these weigh negatively, others positively. As Dr. Russell Barkley has noted, the best adult outcome for hyperactive children, as far as we are aware at this time, appears to be associated with milder hyperactivity, higher intelligence, appropriate parent behavior, and a stable family environment in childhood.

REMEMBER . . .

✦ The majority of hyperactive children become hyperactive teenagers.

✦ Hyperactive teenagers have a high probability of school, social, family, and legal problems.

✦ Hyperactive teenagers with additional conduct problems have the highest likelihood of experiencing these difficulties.

✦ Left untreated, hyperactivity during the teenage years may shape the teenager's personality leading to a lifetime of impulsiveness and self-centeredness.

✦ Hyperactivity, with its resultant weak skills, unreasonable demands, and family structure problems intensifies normal parent–teen problems.

✦ Families with hyperactive teenagers must develop a consistent system of communication, problem solving, and conflict resolution. Working with a professional is usually a necessity, not a luxury.

✦ Some, but not all, hyperactive teenagers grow up to become hyperactive adults.

✦ Hyperactive adults experience greater emotional, social, vocational, and family problems than others.

✦ No single medical or nonmedical treatment in childhood guarantees adult success.

✦ A combination of treatments, higher intelligence, positive family factors, and absence of other disruptive behavior problems, predicts the best adult outcome for hyperactive children.

CHAPTER 9

What Else Can Go Wrong for Hyperactive Children?

Mitchell, Paul, and Susan have each been diagnosed as hyperactive. Mitchell's parents were told that his struggle to master reading was the result of his hyperactivity. Paul is extremely fearful in new situations, he worries that something bad might happen to someone in his family, he has difficulty sleeping, and chooses to play by himself rather than with others. The school psychologist explained to Paul's parents that these problems were not related to his hyperactivity, but the family physician suggested they were. Finally, Susan is rather provocative in her interactions with other children and adults. It is not uncommon for her to run up and kiss another boy in her kindergarten class. She is quite oppositional and often resistant to doing what she is told. Is this part of hyperactivity or are these problems something different?

It has been argued by some that the label hyperactivity is nothing more than a term applied to any disruptive child. Some researchers have argued that the majority of children called hyperactive actually may be depressed. Others suggest that many of these children have anxiety disorders, while still others suggest that the majority are learning disabled or impaired in conduct. Are these hypotheses correct? Probably not. However, it is fair to conclude that having a temperament characterized by inattention, overarousal, restlessness, and impulsiveness from a very early age increases the risk that a child may develop other serious psychological, behavioral, or social problems. Parents also should understand that other groups of children and teenagers with high-risk problems, such as depression, drug or alcohol abuse, may also exhibit many of these adjustment, emotional, behavioral, and developmental problems.

If you are inattentive, eventually you will be accused of not caring. If you are impulsive, eventually people will describe you as self-centered. Finally, if you are easily driven to excesses of emotion and restlessness, adults and other children very quickly become intolerant of your behavior and you find yourself rejected. This explanation should help you make sense of the seemingly illogical pattern of behavior exhibited by hyperactive children. Hyperactivity in and of itself drives adults and children away. In doing so, hyperactivity eventually can have a significant negative impact on the child's emerging personality and self-esteem.

Hyperactive children are at risk to develop other significant childhood problems. Some of these may cause behavior that appears hyperactive. Therefore, we must carefully evaluate the behavior of each hyperactive child to determine whether hyperactivity is the source of the other problems or if the other problems make this child appear hyperactive. Finally, it is possible, that a particular child may have a number of unrelated problems (i.e., hyperactivity and learning disability; or hyperactivity and depression), in combination, that significantly impair the child's ability to deal with the world.

OPPOSITIONAL PROBLEMS

It is not surprising that a large percentage of hyperactive children develop an oppositional pattern. Because their behavior does not meet the expectations of others, they receive a huge dose of negative feedback about the inadequacy or inappropriateness of their actions. Eventually this feedback leads to frustration on the child's part, and the child pushes back in retaliation. Often parents may believe that most of this attitude stems from disobedience, but closer scrutiny frequently reveals that, for most hyperactive children, it results from the child's inability to conform. It would be rare for a child in such a position not to develop some pattern of oppositional behavior. Over time, the mismatch of the child's ability and parental expectations leads to inappropriate demands and escalating punishment. The result is an angry, frustrated child who may become negative, provocative, and oppositional with parents and other authority figures.

Recent research has suggested that as many as 60% of hyperactive children also exhibit oppositional, defiance problems. The essential feature here is a pattern of negative and hostile behavior without the more serious infringements on the basic rights of others that are seen in children with conduct disorders. Oppositional children are argumentative with adults, frequently lose their temper, and seem angry, resentful, or easily annoyed. They often blame others for their mistakes. It is characteristic of oppositional children that this behavior is exhibited more commonly toward adults and children with whom the child interacts on a regular basis. This pattern is rarely seen in a clinical setting with an unfamiliar professional, or in a public setting with adults the child may not know well.

Other characteristics of the oppositional child include losing temper frequently and without provocation, arguing with adults, defying rules, deliberately annoying people, blaming others for mistakes, appearing angry, resentful, spiteful, or using obscene language.

Why does the hyperactive child have a greater probability of developing this oppositional, defiant pattern than other children? Simple. Because the hyperactive child often cannot meet the demands of others, he fails frequently, and as a result becomes frustrated, unhappy, and more negative. For many, a pattern of oppositional behavior does not appear to be a preexisting condition, but develops over time as the result of poor self-control.

A careful review of your child's history will often yield information suggesting that hyperactivity was present well before the child became negative and oppositional. We also believe that it is rare for a child with *just* an oppositional disorder to exhibit sufficient problems with attention span, hyperactivity, and impulsiveness to warrant hyperactivity as an additional diagnosis. Remember, approximately 50 to 70% of hyperactive children are also oppositional.

CONDUCT PROBLEMS

The child with conduct problems appears to take oppositional defiance one step beyond tolerance. This child exhibits behaviors that violate the basic rights of others. Major rules are violated. This is certainly a much more serious problem than simple opposition. Children with conduct problems are often aggressive, cruel, physically violent, destructive of property, and may confront their victims. Many have problems with truancy, drugs, alcohol, and sexual misconduct. Researchers have suggested that at least 30 to 40% of hyperactive children eventually have conduct problems.

As with oppositional problems, it is not surprising that there is a significant overlap between conduct difficulties and hyperactivity. The impulsive behavior of the hyperactive child may result in stealing, lying, or engaging in physical fights. The nonpurposeful, impulsive problems of the hyperactive child may be misinterpreted by many adults as deliberate maliciousness. The child with a serious conduct-disorder, however, is destructive and aggressive with malicious forethought, and consistently engages in activities designed to hurt others for his own gain.

Some children and adolescents with significant conduct problems do not have early histories of hyperactivity. It is safe to say that there is a significant group of children and adolescents with conduct disorders whose problems began with a series of difficulties, including inattention, impulsiveness and overarousal. This group's behavioral problems may have worsened as the result of a mismatch between child and parent temperament; a misinterpretation by parents, teachers, or other authority figures regarding cause; family dysfunction; or a subsequent lack of effective, multidisciplinary intervention. The majority of children or adolescents with conduct disorder and hyperactivity in all likelihood displayed hyperactivity and oppositional problems preceding the onset of serious conduct disorder.

A diagnosis of conduct disorder should be reserved for children and adolescents committing serious and persistent violations of the rights of others. If it is unclear that the hyperactivity is contributing to conduct problems, the child or adolescent with conduct disorder often exhibits a pattern of hyperactivity that is inconsistent across situations. For many conduct-disordered children, reports of hyperactivity may reflect symptoms of their conduct disorder as opposed to symptoms of a separate biological disorder.

Researchers have suggested that some kinds of behaviors may actually distinguish the hyperactive from the conduct-disordered child, others may not. For example, lying and being suspended from school may occur as frequently with conduct disorder as with hyperactivity. However, lying, fire setting and stealing strongly suggest the presence of conduct disorder.

Overall, recent research has found that although hyperactivity and conduct disorder may influence each other, they are separate childhood disorders and probably have different causes and courses of development.

DEPRESSION

Some researchers have suggested that many children diagnosed as hyperactive experience depression or manic depression. Symptoms of hyperactivity have been reported in as many as 60% of depressed children. But hyperactive children also seem to exhibit more sadness, helpless feelings, and lower self-esteem in comparison with normal children because of skill deficiency. Careful scientific research, however, has suggested that the majority of children who are actually depressed display very few symptoms of hyperactivity.

Children having a major depressive episode usually exhibit a change in functioning over a two- or three-week period. During this time one of the primary symptoms observed is either a marked increase in negative mood or a loss of interest or pleasure in activities previously enjoyed. This is an important difference when attempting to determine if a child is exhibiting hyperactivity, depression, or both. The majority of hyperactive problems persist over a long period of time. On this basis alone, the majority of hyperactive children would not be considered as having major depression unless there is a quick, observable, and significant change in their behavior and mood. Characteristic hyperactive symptoms that overlap with depression include difficulty with sleep, irritability, excessive restlessness, impulsive behavior, and difficulty with concentration.

Studies have suggested that as many as 25% of teenagers diagnosed as depressed have earlier histories of hyperactivity. For many of these teenagers, careful assessment usually reveals that hyperactivity eventually resulted in diminished self-esteem and failure—a possible cause of the depression. As we noted in an earlier chapter, approximately 1 out of 4 hyperactives will experience a period of depression in childhood or adolescence. This hyperactivity increases the risk of depression.

Some children are not depressed, they just seem to be always unhappy. These children often have low self-esteem; feel helpless or hopeless; do poorly with friends, family, and at school; and often have problems with sleep, energy level, and appetite. If these symptoms are severe and interspersed between major depressive episodes a diagnosis of dysthymia (chronic unhappiness) may be appropriate. Although many hyperactive children have some of these difficulties, they are clearly neither depressed nor helpless. They simply lack the ability to meet the demands expected by the adults in their lives.

When considering whether the child's problems stem from hyperactivity or depression, a key diagnostic issue is determining the cause of irritable mood; helplessness and unhappiness or simply hyperactive overarousal and impulsiveness. A professional evaluation is essential when depression is suspected. As a parent, carefully recalling your child's development will often provide a definitive answer to this question. The majority of depressed children do not have long histories of inattention or objective test data that clearly reflect an inattention problem. Hyperactive children with a long history of environmental failure appear at greatest risk for developing chronic, depressive problems.

ANXIETY

Problems with anxiety in childhood often involve difficulty separating from parents, avoidance of others, or excessive worry about specific events. Parents and professionals insensitive to the restless, seemingly anxious behavior of the hyperactive child risk interpreting behavior, including pulling of clothing, wiping an arm back and forth across a desk, or fidgeting in a chair as signs of excessive anxiety. In fact, they are symptoms of hyperactivity. The reverse may also be true. In general, however, for the hyperactive child, apparent nervousness is related to a physical state that occurs steadily and is often independent of events in the environment.

Children with anxiety disorders typically have excessive physical complaints, are self-conscious, have an excessive need for reassurance, and feel tense or unable to relax. They may worry about themselves, their family, and the future. Their problems and the manifestations of their behavioral difficulties are very different from the problems of the hyperactive child. Nonetheless, some research has suggested that children described as inattentive, but not necessarily restless, overactive, or impulsive may actually have some form of anxiety disorder and are not hyperactive.

It is uncommon for a hyperactive child to develop serious, anxiety-related symptoms. Research, however, has suggested that as many as 25% of hyperactive children and adolescents may experience some anxiety-related symptoms and may ultimately receive a diagnosis of anxiety disorder. Usually these symptoms reflect worry or concern about school and social success. It is also rare for the child with significant anxiety problems to have the range of attention and activity level problems that characterize most hyperactive children. When symptoms of anxiety are present, a professional evaluation is essential.

ADJUSTMENT PROBLEMS

A period of emotional unrest or distress occurs in anyone's life when the person is faced with significant stress. Stress can result from the loss of a loved one, a change of schools, or a traumatic experience (i.e., accident). Adjustment difficulties usually last from three to six months. They may impair a child's ability to function at school and socially, and may vary from child to child but represent a clear change for the worse in the child's overall functioning.

Some children experiencing adjustment problems appear to demonstrate more symptoms in one or another area, such as depression, anxiety, physical complaints, or difficulty with conduct. Many hyperactive children in response to school stress may develop a pattern of emotional difficulty. Frequently, these problems are not severe enough to warrant a diagnosis of depression, anxiety, or conduct problems. The symptoms, however, represent a change for the worse in the child's adjustment. In this particular case, the specific stresses that set off this change in adjustment are the demands of school. The hyperactive child's adjustment problems frequently worsen as school begins and improve when summer starts. These problems reflect the number of forces acting on the hyperactive child and the child's inability to cope adequately with them. As summer brings fewer demands, many hyperactive children function better. Once school begins again and the failure builds up, they again demonstrate increasing emotional difficulty.

By definition, adjustment problems do not represent a long-term pattern of disability. It is therefore rare for a child experiencing only adjustment problems to appear as if he had a history of hyperactivity. As with many other disorders of childhood, hyperactive children with adjustment disorders stemming from a specific stress, such a death in the immediate family, usually have a preexisting pattern of hyperactive problems. However, the adjustment difficulties arise from the new demands placed on the hyperactive child, not from hyperactivity.

LANGUAGE PROBLEMS

Researchers have suggested that as children with serious speech and language problems grow, many develop patterns of inattentive and hyperactive behavior. Some studies have suggested that as many as two thirds of preschool and one third of school age language-impaired children also experience problems consistent with hyperactivity. Many of these children develop these patterns of behavior in response to the stress and frustration arising from their difficulty communicating.

As young children develop language, they also develop the ability to control themselves. As verbal abilities improve, children are able to understand their world and express their needs more effectively, and language becomes a substitute for action. When language development is abnormal, the development of self-control is disrupted. It is important to understand the critical link between language development and appropriate behavior. Children with language impairments are frequently placed in situations in which they cannot effectively respond, not because of a lack of motivation or even hyperactivity, but because of specific language disability. When parents and teachers inadvertently continue to place pressure on the language-disordered child to conform behaviorally, that child may develop a long-term pattern of behavior problems consistent with those observed in hyperactive children. Parents' frustration concerning a language-impaired child's inability to follow directions may lead to anger and exacerbate the child's frustration. This leads to further misbehavior and temper tantrums on the part of the child.

During the preschool years, many language impairments may go unrecognized by parents and many professionals. Frequently, the child's misbehavior ends up being the focus of treatment and results in intervention directed at improving symptomatic behavior rather than the child's language skills. As hyperactivity has become an increasingly popular subject, it is also more likely that many parents may perceive the behavior of their language-impaired child as stemming from this biological disorder rather than from the child's frustration and inability to communicate.

Because of the overlap between language disability and hyperactivity, careful professional assessment is necessary to understand the source of the behavior and the areas in need of remediation. Many 2- and 3-year-olds who appear hyperactive but who also have significant language problems, demonstrate significant improvements in their behavior when an appropriate course of language therapy and parent training is provided.

With school-aged children, language processing impairments are far more subtle. Processing of language refers to the child's ability to understand what has been said so these problems may be difficult to detect. The frustrated, older language-impaired child who appears hyperactive may not demonstrate significant problems with attention span on structured tests or when appropriate instructions are provided prior to task completion. Also, this child usually seems to have much greater problems with auditory as opposed to visual attention. Preschoolers exhibiting hyperactivity should routinely have their language development screened. When language problems are suspected in older children, a speech pathologist should be consulted.

AUDITORY PROCESSING PROBLEMS

Effective hearing involves not only the ability to hear sounds but to transmit auditory information from the ear to the brain effectively. Impairment in this system can result in poor auditory attention, difficulty understanding speech, limitations in auditory memory, and delayed language development.

At home or in the classroom, children with specific auditory processing problems related to attention and memory may appear to have many of the same symptoms as hyperactive children. They are inattentive and seem easily distracted. But often, they are not excessively emotional, impulsive, or overactive.

Some researchers have suggested that auditory processing problems in children are actually a part of hyperactivity. There is a heated debate among audiologists, and lines of opinion are clearly drawn. We believe that hyperactivity and poor auditory processing are two very different disorders that may, at times, present similar symptoms. If your child is described as inattentive, but not hyperactive, screening for auditory processing problems should be considered.

MEMORY PROBLEMS

In order to remember, a child must pay attention. If a child has difficulty remembering, it may appear as if he does not pay attention. Hyperactive children will not process as much information and therefore will not have the opportunity to store and recall as much information as others. Frequently, hyperactive children appear to have memory deficiencies. Children with memory disorders, because of their poor recall, are often accused of not paying attention well. Differentiating between these problems is often a difficult task, even for the professional.

Memory is an extremely complex process. Professionals make a distinction between auditory and visual memory as well as between immediate, short-term and long-term memory. Some experts even argue that because memory is so important for all neurological tasks, it cannot be accurately measured in and of itself but only in relation to other things. Often we infer the quality of a child's memory skills based on a variety of auditory, visual, and motor tasks. Children with memory difficulty, but not hyperactivity, will exhibit lower scores on hyperactive checklists and minimal social and situational problems. They usually perform well on tasks requiring persistence and do not demonstrate the often inconsistent and unpredictable course of the hyperactive child.

LEARNING PROBLEMS

Learning-impaired children, frustrated because of years of academic failure, may exhibit problems that mimic hyperactivity.

These children, however, usually do not have a preschool history of behavior consistent with hyperactivity. In addition, on direct assessment in a one-on-one setting, the learning-disabled child does not appear to demonstrate the level of distractibility and impulsiveness characteristic of the hyperactive child. Some researchers have suggested that hyperactive children with and without learning disabilities experience problems sustaining attention. However, learning-disabled children who are not hyperactive do not have problems sustaining attention, but have greater difficulty deciding what to pay attention to and remembering the information they are attending to.

Difficulty controlling emotions, excessive activity, and inattention may be characteristic symptoms of frustration resulting from the learning-disabled child's inability to meet the demands of school. Careful evaluation of this group of children, however, often reveals that in nonschool settings they do not have the range of hyperactive symptoms characteristic of the typical hyperactive child. Many hyperactive children may not perform well at school, but they are capable of learning. It is important to recognize, however, that approximately 10 to 30% of hyperactive children also experience learning disabilities. Academic achievement should be evaluated as part of the multidisciplinary evaluation for hyperactivity.

INTELLIGENCE

Although intelligence and attention span are not closely related, it is fair to say that children with fewer intellectual skills, especially those in the handicapped range, are simply not as stimulated by events in their environment and therefore do not pay attention as well. For this group, difficulty with attention is a symptom of faulty intelligence. When evaluated, these children appear to have all the situational and skill problems characteristic of the typical hyperactive child. The majority of these children, however, do not experience primary attention deficiency. When their behavior and skills are compared with their mental age, they do not seem to have problems that differ significantly from other intellectually handicapped children.

Among the population of mildly intellectually deficient children, there are some for whom paying attention and controlling emotions and bodily movement are significant hurdles. This small population of intellectually handicapped/hyperactive children may certainly experience both kinds of problems. Treatment for this group's hyperactivity must be approached with caution. These children, however, can benefit from both medical and nonmedical treatment just the same as intellectually competent children.

SPECIFIC COGNITIVE PROBLEMS

Some children may have normal preschool and early elementary histories but by second grade demonstrate an increasing pattern of what appears to be late onset hyperactivity. Such children are not truly hyperactive, but rather have a specific learning disability that interferes more with the child's ability to function effectively in the classroom than with reading, spelling, and mathematics. Some psychologists refer to these problems as stemming from weaknesses in executive skills such as reasoning, organizing, and decision making. As one parent informed the authors, up through first grade children learn to read. By second grade, they must read to learn. Unfortunately, when this transaction takes places, some children have difficulty with the speed at which they can learn new information, the skills with which they can organize that information, the formation of new concepts, and the ability to think flexibly or solve problems effectively.

These children seem to do well up through first grade. By second grade, the amount of information they must learn daily increases dramatically and they slowly fall behind. They must pay attention and handle new tasks each day. An inability to handle these tasks often results in frustration and then an increase in what appear to be hyperactive problems.

When the histories of these children are carefully reviewed, it is clear they did not exhibit hyperactive problems before first grade.

Careful assessment also reveals that these children are not actually inattentive, excessively restless, or impulsive, but rather extremely frustrated because their cognitive problems interfere with their ability to succeed at school.

OTHER MEDICAL PROBLEMS

In Chapter 3, we discussed physical symptoms that may mimic hyperactivity but are the result of an unrelated medical illness. Your pediatrician or family physician can quickly evaluate and rule out hyperthyroidism, sleep apnea, infection with pinworms, and otitis media. Although most of these disorders occur rarely and seldom cause symptoms consistent with a full syndrome of hyperactivity, they must be considered as part of the hyperactivity evaluation.

REMEMBER . . .

✦ Symptoms of inattention, overanxiety, and impulsiveness share common ground with many childhood disorders. While the majority of children exhibiting these symptoms also exhibit hyperactivity, some may not. For this small group of children, their symptoms of hyperactivity may stem from medical, educational, emotional or behavioral problems.

✦ In addition, hyperactive children appear at greater risk than others for secondary, learning, behavioral, and even medical problems. In some situations, the hyperactivity is related to these problems, while in others the relationship may be minimal. For this reason a thorough evaluation by a trained professional is essential for all children suspected of being hyperactive.

✦ If your child demonstrates a pattern of resistant, oppositional behavior, or acts toward others in a way that violates their rights, assessment is necessary to determine whether this behavior stems from hyperactivity, contributes to hyperactivity, or actually reflects a secondary disruptive problem.

✦ If your child suddenly develops a change in sleep or appetite, and is more moody and unhappy, some type of depression may exist. Remember, hyperactive children may have feelings of helplessness and low self-esteem as the result of their repeated failure. They usually do not demonstrate sudden, marked changes in their overall behavior and mood.

✦ If your child has repeated physical complaints; is quite self-conscious; reports feeling tense; and worries about himself, family members, and the future, an anxiety disorder should be suspected.

✦ When a major change creates stress in the family, such as loss of a loved one, children have periods of grief and adjustment. These periods can be accompanied by behavior that often resembles hyperactivity.

✦ There is a very close relationship between language mastery and self-control. Children with language problems risk developing disruptive behavior symptoms that resemble hyperactivity.

✦ Children with learning and related problems may struggle to achieve academically and may also have difficulty with memory or problem solving that interferes with daily classroom performance. The majority of these children, however, are not hyperactive.

PART III

WHAT CAN PARENTS DO?

CHAPTER 10

The Impossible Dream: Four Steps to Successful Parenting

In kindergarten, Joseph was restless, inattentive, and experienced great difficulty fitting into the school routine. He experienced similar problems at home. On the advice of the teacher, Joseph's parents spoke with their pediatrician, who recognized signs of hyperactivity and temperamental difficulty in Joseph. After carefully evaluating Joseph's medical status, he referred the family to a psychologist who specialized in hyperactive children. Following careful assessment, Joseph's strengths and weaknesses were identified. In addition to temperamental problems consistent with hyperactivity, the assessment identified a specific language disability that was interfering with Joseph's ability to understand and follow instructions in class. Joseph's educational team, his pediatrician, and the community-based psychologist worked together to develop a plan of medical and nonmedical interventions for Joseph. Joseph's parents participated in a parent-training program in which they learned to understand, recognize, and deal effectively with Joseph's incompetent and at times noncompliant behavioral problems. A classroom response-cost and behavior management program was initiated. Joseph also began working with a language therapist. The psychologist worked briefly with Joseph, helping him understand the reasons for his current difficulties and making

137

certain that he was an active as opposed to a resistant or passive participant in his treatment. As nonmedical intervention was initiated, Joseph's physician kept in touch with the educational team and psychologist. Subsequently, stimulant medication was tried with great success. Now in second grade, Joseph is doing well socially, academically, emotionally, and behaviorally. Although he continues to experience hyperactivity and at times is a challenge for his parents and teachers, Joseph is happy and well adjusted. His parents feel comfortable and competent in their ability to manage his behavior.

FOUR STEPS TO SUCCESS

Step One: Understanding

The initial and most important step in raising your hyperactive child effectively is acquiring education and understanding. Many books and programs for parents teach techniques at the expense of understanding. Parents become dependent on a handful of techniques or on a parent-training manual and are unable to think for themselves.

A variety of parent-training programs can be helpful when dealing with hyperactive children. Success, however, may be short-lived. For long-term success you must develop an understanding of your child's behavior and an awareness of the ways in which you interact with your child. You must be sensitive to the long-term effects hyperactivity is going to have on your child.

As a parent, it is important for you to see the world through the eyes of your hyperactive child. This will help you cope on a daily basis, because your hyperactive child, as the result of temperament may present an unending series of problems.

Parents need to understand their own temperaments as well. If you are impulsive and frustrate quickly these traits will have a negative influence on your ability to help your child.

The following questionnaire will help you recognize temperamental qualities consistent with hyperactivity that you as an adult may possess. Take a moment and complete the questionnaire. Again, as with the questionnaires in Chapter 2, there is no score. However, if your response is yes to many of these items, you should be aware that your own temperament may conflict with that of your child.

ADULT TEMPERAMENT QUESTIONNAIRE

I am:	Yes	No
Always on the go.	_____	_____
Restless.	_____	_____
Easily distracted.	_____	_____
Short tempered.	_____	_____
Moody.	_____	_____
Disorganized.	_____	_____
Frequently acting without thinking.	_____	_____
Frequently losing control of my temper.	_____	_____
Impulsive.	_____	_____
Inattentive.	_____	_____
Easily bored.	_____	_____

Step Two: Distinguishing Between Noncompliance or Incompetence

In the first chapter of this book, we explained the difference between incompetence and noncompliance. Incompetent behavior results when a child does not possess the skills to succeed. Noncompliant behavior results when a child chooses to behave in a certain way regardless of the consequences. Problems of incompetence must be treated with education and skill building. Problems of noncompliance are best firmly, consistently, and appropriately punished.

Most of the problems hyperactive children have result from incompetence. The hyperactive child's difficulties in starting a task, sticking to it, becoming overemotional and easily frustrated, acting impulsively, or being excessively restless cause a variety of unintentional problems. Unfortunately, these problems are disturbing to all those around the child. It is important as adults to understand that our response to this pattern of annoying behavior often results in an endless stream of quit it, stop it, cut it out and don't do that responses. As a result of this type of feedback, the hyperactive child risks looking at his or her world as negative and controlling. This pattern then leads to further resistant, oppositional, and noncompliant behavior. By successfully distinguishing between incompetent and noncompliant behavior, you can reduce negative feedback and increase your child's compliance and success, and successfully avoid the development of oppositional behavior.

If you punish your child for an impulsive response, there is a strong likelihood that your child will be sorry and promise to behave better. Unfortunately, if your child is hyperactive, the next time the situation arises the child's impulsive need to act will outweigh his capacity to stop, think, and plan, and the problem will reoccur. It is critical that as a parent you understand this. You would not punish your 7-year-old if he were unable to read, expecting punishment to increase his reading ability. Instead you would spend time teaching your child to read by developing a basic foundation of reading skills. Parents of hyperactive children must understand that punishing inattentive, impersistent, restless, overemotional, or impulsive behavior stands little chance of changing that behavior.

Step Three: Give Positive Directions

It is necessary for you to become proficient at differentiating between incompetent and noncompliant behavior. It is also important to determine the source of the child's problems because noncompliant behavior will be punished while incompetence must be dealt with through education and skill building. When you try to distinguish between incompetent and noncompliant behavior, you may be frequently frustrated. The third step to success, providing positive directions, may help you recognize this difference.

Human nature appears to direct each of us to point out what we dislike, rather than what we like, about something. When a child exhibits negative behavior, most parents respond by directing the child to stop doing it. Focusing on what should be stopped, as opposed to what should be started, results in the hyperactive child's receiving a steady diet of negative directions. This does not help the child understand what he should do.

For example, if your child has his feet on the wall and you tell him to take them off the wall, you are providing him with a negative instruction. Although it sounds as if you are telling the child what to do, you are really telling him what not to do. This leaves him with a range of possibilities. He may then take his feet off the wall and place them on the coffee table. The child has complied with your request but is now doing something else that is likely to provoke your anger. and the problem may escalate. You may then tell your child to take his feet off the coffee table only to have him place them on the bookcase.

Another experience, as reported by a colleague, describes a child punished for saying the word *shit*. His mother scolded him and warned him to not say this word. This was an intelligent child. In an effort to meet the social demands of his friends, he found a word in the dictionary that sounded similar, *ship*. Using the word ship would allow him to fit into his social group and comply with his mother's directions. He had no desire to be further punished. Unfortunately, his mother had some difficulty hearing and could not tell the difference between the two words. The child was again punished. The problem is his mother's because the child was directed what to not say, as opposed to what to say, when he became angry or frustrated.

It is important for parents to learn to tell their children what they want to have happen instead of what they don't want to have happen. Practice telling your children what you want instead of what you don't want for at least a week. This sounds like an easy task. It is not. Old habits are difficult to change. Many parents find themselves focusing on what they want stopped without considering the nature of the child's actions. Some parents get frustrated and report that it is easy to observe what they don't want the child to do, but much more difficult to decide quickly what they want the child to do. A good rule is to ask yourself what you want to see your child doing instead of what he is doing right now.

Consistently telling your child what to do instead of what not to do may make a very positive change in his behavior. Instead of telling your child to stop running, instruct him to walk. Instead of telling him to stop screaming, instruct him to speak in an inside voice. Instead of telling him to stop writing on the walls, tell him to write in his coloring book.

Giving positive directions can help you make the distinction between incompetence and noncompliance. If you gain your child's attention and instruct him to place his feet on the floor, and he does not comply within 15 seconds, his lack of follow-through usually has nothing to do with hyperactivity, but rather reflects noncompliance. At that point, a brief, immediate punishment may prove beneficial in the long run and increase compliance when you give your child directions.

It is also important for you to understand that once you make a request of your child, you must remain to see what happens. Suppose, you ask your child to place his feet on the floor, but you walk out of the room. If when you come back 10 minutes later your child has his feet on the wall, you cannot be certain whether this is a problem of incompetence or noncompliance. You have no idea whether the child complied for a few moments and was distracted, or did not comply at all. You must remain until the child complies. But what should you do if the child complies but 10 minutes later again has his feet on the wall? The following example will help you deal with this problem.

One of the keys to improving the hyperactive child's behavior at home is the parents' consistent management of the environment in order to minimize the child's problems. In many situations, you may have to act as a control system for your child. This will reduce negative confrontations and the escalation of problems. For example, if your child is playing with a friend and he becomes overly loud, you must provide a positive direction for the child to speak in an inside voice. In most situations, the child may comply for a few moments but 10 minutes later, because he does not track the volume of his voice, he is loud again. Usually in this situation, parents become angry, and by the third offense the child is sent to his room and the friend is sent home.

As a parent of a hyperactive child, however, you must make the distinction between incompetence and noncompliance. If you ask the child to lower his voice and he complies for a period of time but then his voice gradually becomes louder again, this is not the result of noncompliance. In all likelihood, this reflects the child's inability to control the volume of his voice. You must then make another positive direction and request that the child speak in an inside voice. In that way, you are acting as a control system for your child. During a one-hour play session you may have to remind your child a number of times to speak in an inside voice. The question you must ask yourself is, what happens after the request is made? If your child complies, then he is making an attempt to meet your request. If over time your child has a problem again, it is most likely the result of incompetence and therefore the child is entitled to another positive direction. In this situation, the result is a number of small successes rather than one large failure.

Now that you have effectively managed the child's problems, it is time to initiate an educational or cognitive intervention. You may instruct your child that it would be great if he could remember to follow the direction for more than a few minutes. However, you are aware that the child is not doing this on purpose and you will remind the child so long as he is compliant when the reminder is made. You may then suggest setting a timer to ring every 5 or 10 minutes. If the child is speaking in an inside voice when the timer goes off, a point may be earned. If enough points are earned during a playtime, some reward will be given to both the child and his friend at the end of the playtime. The use of a timer and reward increases your child's motivation and ability to keep track of the volume of his voice on his own. Thus this intervention increases your child's competence.

Step Four: Fostering Success

Hyperactive children have long histories of failure. Typically, the child creates a problem, is punished, and rarely has the opportunity to return to the situation and succeed. If a problem results from noncompliance, it is essential after punishment that the child return to the problem situation and comply with your original request. The message to your child must be very clear. Regardless of the time involved, he will eventually comply with your requests. For this reason, it is best to provide brief periods of punishment designed to give the child the message that you are dissatisfied and to return him quickly to the problem situation.

Studies have found that hyperactive children have many more negative interactions with parents and teachers than other children. It is important for your child to succeed even when he is noncompliant. Give a positive direction, deal with noncompliance in a consistent, brief fashion, and most importantly, find ways to praise your child.

Most children, when punished for inappropriate behavior and rewarded for more appropriate behavior, will eventually improve. When consequences are withdrawn, most children maintain the positive behavioral change. The child internalizes the change in behavior. Hyperactive children frequently lack the ability to successfully internalize and develop responsibility for their own behavior. Therefore, they may perform well under a system of structured reinforcement but be unable to maintain those changes without it. You must understand the difference between incompetence and noncompliance, as well as that your hyperactive child's problems need to be managed throughout his childhood. This will make it easier for you to recognize the need to continue providing a significant degree of structure and management. Those interventions are essential for your child to maintain positive behavior changes.

Styles of Parent Intervention

Most parents of hyperactive children quickly realize that how to manuals or six-week parent-training courses are insufficient to meet the needs of their children. Being an effective parent for a hyperactive child is a multistep process. You must first understand how and why your hyperactive child behaves the way he does, and the role you play as you interact with your child. Your temperament and choice of interventions will affect your child not only today but throughout his lifetime. As parents you have a menu from which to choose your responses. Parents attempt to reduce or eliminate their children's problems in either preventive (before the problem occurs) or reactionary ways (after the problem occurs). In both situations, you may choose to manage the environment or change the child. This combination results in four alternative levels of parental behavior. These are illustrated in Figure 10–1. First, you may anticipate a problem and teach your child a more competent skill. Second, you may prevent something by manipulating the environment to reduce the chances that the problem will occur. Third, you can react after the problem has occurred and try to manipulate the environment to reduce the chance that the problem will recur. Finally, you can react and either punish the child or teach him skills that will help him gain better control over his behavior.

Consider for a moment what you do when your hyperactive child has a problem. What do you do when he is repeatedly unable to sit still in a restaurant, doesn't stick to assigned chores at home, or can't settle down to bed? The odds are that you attempt to punish or use a negative reinforcement. The odds are also that your behavior occurs in reaction to the problem.

In the style of that popular game show, "Family Feud," the primary parent response to childhood problems is reactionary—punishment designed to change the child's behavior. For most children, this is a successful intervention. Unfortunately, for the incompetent, skill deficient, hyperactive child, a punishment is usually ineffective. It neither improves the child's ability nor his chance of succeeding the next time. It is critical for parents of hyperactive

FIGURE 10-1 What Can Parents Do? Points of Parental Response. The Problem: Child getting into kitchen cabinets.

PREVENTIVE LEVELS

Modifying the Environment

"The locks on the cabinets will keep you out of trouble."

Modifying the Child

"You've done a good job learning which cabinets not to open. I have a reward for you."

REACTIVE LEVELS

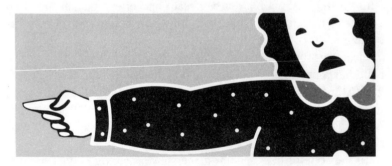

Modifying the Environment

"I am sick and tired of you making a mess in the cabinets. Get out of the kitchen."

Modifying the Child

"I am going to punish you for getting into the kitchen cabinets again. Maybe time-out in your room will help you remember to stay out of the cabinets."

children to understand that repeated and increasingly reactionary, often punishing, measures, will not help. This pattern of parental response usually *increases* behavioral problems.

Children are not masochistic. They do not wake up in the morning and set out to make their lives and yours miserable. If, over repeated situations, reactive punishments are ineffective, you must consider that the problem may be incompetence and be willing to consider alternatives.

The younger your hyperactive child, the more successful you will be if you direct your efforts at controlling the environment by prevention. With an older child it is much more difficult to control the environment so interventions directed at the child and designed to teach skills or punish inappropriate, noncompliant behavior, are often more effective. Two-year-olds are much easier to control than 6- or 10-year-olds. Your ability to anticipate problems and act to prevent them by controlling your child's environment will help avoid escalation and the frustrating pattern of increasingly punitive measures.

Keep in mind that there are always alternative responses available when your hyperactive child misbehaves. If you react and are not successful, continuing in the same manner will frustrate both you and your child.

STRATEGIES THAT HELP

Time Out

Go to your room is probably the most frequent command parents give when they are frustrated or unhappy with their child's behavior. Being isolated, away from others, is a time-out intervention, which by definition, is a punishment. Time out is one of the most popular forms of parental discipline. Although positive forms of discipline, such as rewarding appropriate behavior, are certainly preferable, punishment when used appropriately is very effective for noncompliant behavior.

Time out is very effective for children between the ages of 4 and 12. Unfortunately, many parents may not be successful with it because while sending the child to his room may restrict him from the rest of the house, it may allow him to watch TV, play video games, or engage in other fun activities.

It is important for time out to be a punishment—to let the child know you are unhappy with his actions. For time out to be effective, you must follow up with instruction and quickly bring your child back to the problem situation, and again request that he comply. Time out is used for noncompliance. It is not very useful for incompetence. For example, if a child cannot read, sending him to his room or placing him in a chair will not improve his reading ability.

When your child is noncompliant, as in the case of not moving his feet to the floor, he should be sent immediately to time out. The time-out chair can be in the same room as the offense, preferably facing a wall or corner. The only requirement is that the child's bottom remain in the chair. A child may cry or talk to himself but he may not do anything entertaining such as playing with toys, talking to others, watching television or listening to music. The time-out period should be brief—as short as one minute. This is such a short amount of time that even the most hyperactive child can easily comply and control himself if he so chooses. This brief time out also allows your child to return quickly to the problem situation and again try to comply.

It is important for you to be firm concerning time out. Do not ask your child if time out is needed. If it is needed, recommend it and do it *now*. Don't let your child bargain with you once you say that it is necessary. Do not lecture, scream, or scold your child on the way to time out. Finally, do not promise time out if you cannot enforce it.

The purpose of time out is to let your child know when he is being noncompliant and allow him to return quickly to make another attempt. The purpose is not to make your child feel bad or to make you feel better. When your child returns to the situation, the reason for time out is briefly stated and the direction is again given. If we return to our original problem, the child may be directed to place his feet on the floor. If the child's feet remain on the floor for the next 10 to 15 seconds you may end the interaction with a positive reinforcer—thank the child for following instructions. If 15 minutes later your child's feet are on the wall again, your first impulse will be annoyance and anger. For the hyperactive child, however, a second positive direction must be given. The distinction must always be made between noncompliance and incompetence. If your child responds appropriately when a direction is given, a verbal reinforcer such as "good job" is offered. If the child again refuses, time out is again initiated. The child starts again at the same level of time out, one minute.

If your hyperactive child is trying to pick a fight with you and be oppositional, he may come out of time out and still refuse to follow your instruction. It is easy for you at that point to recognize that this is deliberate behavior that must be punished. There is no need for a positive statement. Send the child back to time out and add one minute. In this way, even in repeated negative situations time out does not turn into an all-afternoon affair. Once your child returns from time out, you again provide a positive instruction and wait for compliance. If the child does not comply, the interaction continues and another minute of time out is added. This is a battle that your child cannot win. Eventually your child will comply and be reinforced. Once that happens you may explain to the child that he is in control of his behavior, but sooner or later he will comply. It is certainly easier for everyone when he complies sooner. Time spent working toward compliance could be spent doing something much more enjoyable.

Many parents become frustrated when the child refuses to go to or stay in time out. Psychologist Dr. Tom Phelan describes the six kinds of behavior children exhibit to test parents' decisions, including those concerning time out. It is helpful for you to recognize when your child engages in these behaviors and understand that they are designed to get you to back off. Children will:

1. Badger (i.e., why can't I, please, when?).
2. Attempt to intimidate you (i.e., bang on doors, yell, throw things).
3. Threaten (i.e., I won't talk to you again, I am going to run away from home).

4. Play the martyr (i.e., cry, pout, look sad, or depressed).
5. Try to be overly sweet and nice (i.e., try to get you to give in because they are so nice).
6. Resort to physical means (i.e., attack you or physically run away).

If your child refuses to go to time out or attempts to change the subject by throwing a tantrum or engaging in other testing behaviors, *don't* pay attention to him. Many parents ignore. They ignore the good, the bad, and just about everything else their children do. Ignoring is an active process. To ignore effectively, you must not pay attention to behavior you do not like, but immediately pay positive attention when the child begins to behave better. In most situations, however, once you make a direct request of the child and he is noncompliant, ignoring will not be effective. However, when you request your child follow through with a punishment such as time out, and the child tries to manipulate you by throwing a tantrum, ignoring it provides him with a clear message that you will not deal with him when he is inappropriate or noncompliant. When the child regains self-control, return to the situation, reinforce your child for being in control, and again direct the child to follow through with the punishment.

Again, this process is a battle your child cannot win. Although some children may repeatedly test it, most quickly recognize that sooner or later they will have to go to time out. When by the third time you return, your child is still noncompliant, it is suggested that you add an additional punishment such as earlier bedtime or no television if your child does not go to time out on the next request. It is rare that a child will continue to be noncompliant when you promise a second punishment.

If your child gets out of the time out chair before the minute is over, ask him to return to the chair and instruct him that if he leaves the chair a second time the clock will be started over and he will be given one spank. For younger children, a clap of your hands is often an effective accompaniment to the word spank. Some parents are uncomfortable using even a single spank, and this component is not essential. However, if you are unwilling to spank your child, do not threaten to do so. If you are going to use a spank it is suggested that this be the only situation in which you use it so that its effectiveness is maintained. Spanking means business. Each subsequent time the child leaves the chair one spank is given and the clock is started over again. Regardless of the number of times a child leaves the chair, only one spank is given and no penalty time other than starting the clock over is added to time out. Spanking should also not become a daily intervention. If you must use it daily, it is ineffective. Find other nonphysical ways of letting your child know you mean business. Remember, hyperactive children have difficulty with any task requiring persistence. They will have equal difficulty complying with lengthy punishments.

We do not recommend dragging older children to time out or restraining them in the time-out chair. One reason our prisons do not often rehabilitate is that most individuals in prison believe they are there because they were caught, convicted, and placed behind bars. They are not remorseful nor do they perceive their behavior to be the problem. If you physically restrain your child as a punishment, your child will place the blame on you and not on his behavior. If, on the other hand, your child is sitting voluntarily in the time-out chair, his willingness to comply is an acknowledgment of inappropriate behavior and the chances that punishment will be effective increase.

Some children, unfortunately, may be unwilling to accept any form of intervention. Such children may continue to escalate their resistance and opposition until they have a major tantrum, are out of control, and get you out of control. Such children may require a safe, padded, illuminated, ventilated, time-out booth. In such situations, it is suggested that you seek professional help in making decisions about constructing it. This may be necessary if less restrictive forms of time out are not accepted by the child. In most cases, the child tests your resolve once or twice and then no longer escalates his negative behavior to the point where the booth is necessary. Unfortunately, some children do not even benefit from a time-out booth. These children frequently are experiencing many more problems than just hyperactivity and are in need of professional help and possibly placement in special out of home programs.

Positive Practice

If your child slams the door, your response should be a positive instruction such as: Doors must be shut quietly. Unless your child happens to be going through another door immediately, there is no opportunity to assess the issue of noncompliance versus incompetence. Most parents, in such situations, have the child return and go through the door again in an appropriate manner. When this process is repeated a number of times, it is referred to as positive practice. It is a good intervention for incompetent behavior. In such a situation, you must approach the child with a smile and make it very clear that this is not punishment but practice. If we do not read well, we practice. If we do not kick a soccer ball well, we practice. Therefore if we do not close doors well, we practice. Have the child practice 10 times consecutively walking through the door in an appropriate way. This will increase the chances that the next time the child goes through a door, he will remember what to do and act appropriately.

It may also be helpful to explain to the child that if the door is slammed the next time, this simply means there was not enough practice this time. Next time, the number of practice sessions will be doubled. Practicing appropriate behavior is an excellent intervention for building skills. It works well with a wide range of behaviors including forgetting to flush the toilet, hang up a coat, or wash hands before dinner.

Response-Cost

Most parents understand the use of positive reinforcers or rewards as means of motivating children. Few, however, understand the use of response-cost. Response-cost is a form of punishment. You may lose what you earn. You may give the child a dollar for good work but penalize him a quarter for poor work.

Hyperactive children, as the result of their temperament problems, do not earn as many rewards as other children. Therefore, they find it difficult to be motivated by rewards they think they can never obtain. For hyperactive children it is suggested that you modify response-cost to provide the child with the entire reward at the beginning. The child must then work to keep the reward. Instead of giving the child a $2.00 allowance at the end of the week you may place the $2.00 in nickels in a jar on a shelf that is visible to your child. So long as your child behaves appropriately the $2.00 belongs to him. Every time there is an infraction that has been clearly defined and agreed on between you and your child, a nickel is removed from the jar. Hyperactive children, because of their histories of negative reinforcement and inability to earn rewards, seem to perform much better when they are working to keep what they already have rather than to earn something that they do not have.

Negative Reinforcement

Earlier we explained negative reinforcement. It is important for you to understand the powerful effect negative reinforcement has on your hyperactive child. Over time your child develops a view of the world in which he is repeatedly working to get rid of things that he does not like rather than to earn things which he likes. It may be difficult to break this cycle. If you are going to use negative reinforcement, you must use it in a constructive manner. If you send your child off to complete an activity, repeatedly check on the child after short periods. This increases the chances that when you check, the child will be engaged in the task and you can then provide a positive reinforcer. If the child is not on task, you must remain with the child until the task is *completed*. You do not yell, harass, or converse with the child. You supervise. Although this, too, is negative reinforcement, in this situation the child learns that the only way to get rid of your negative attention is not just to start the task but to complete it.

Self-Monitoring

Most of us learn to track our own behavior. We check the clock, the calendar, or the date book. We develop the ability to estimate the amount of work to be completed and the time needed to complete it. Hyperactive children, however, struggle to develop these skills.

Self-monitoring is a technique that provides the hyperactive child with a cue to assist him in learning to monitor himself. For example, during a play period, instead of coming in and directing the child to speak in an inside voice you can set a timer to ring every 10 minutes. You instruct the child that he is to make certain he is speaking in an inside voice and following the rules when the timer rings. He then is to reset the timer and return to play.

Self-monitoring can be used in a variety of situations including helping children with morning routines. You and your child can cooperate to structure a schedule of required activities and the time allotted to complete them. Then have the child make an audio tape in which he tells himself what he is supposed to be doing at that moment. That tape may also include a favorite song recorded between each instruction. Each morning you come in and start the tape. The tape acts as an external cue helping your child complete all necessary morning activities.

Psychologist Dr. Harvey Parker has developed a self-regulation program for children that teaches them to use self-monitoring to establish better control over their own behavior and attention (see Appendix). Through the use of a tape player and a signaling tape, children learn to remain on task and return themselves to task during class and homework. (More information is available about this program from IMPACT Publications, 300 N.W. 70th Ave., Suite 102, Plantation, Florida 33317.)

The Punishment Should Fit the Crime

Often, the partial loss of a privilege or possession is a better punishment than complete loss. Remember, hyperactive children have a long history of earning few rewards and losing many privileges. So the loss of another one may have very little meaning or long-term impact. Arranging punishment so that all is not lost as the result of one infraction provides the opportunity for the child to receive at least partial reward. For example, if your child is 10 minutes late for dinner, rather than completely restricting his going out the next day, making him come home 15 or 20 minutes earlier is a better intervention.

Instead of taking away your child's entire allowance, take half or two thirds and leave the child with enough money so he has something to spend, but not enough to purchase all that he may want. Your child's mind-set is important. Rather than having your child approach a situation saying he has nothing and simply forgetting about it, your child has something but not quite enough to get what he wants. This may stimulate more thought and increase the likelihood that he will benefit from this punishment.

Dealing with Sibling Rivalry

For whatever reason, as parents we assume that an older child should take more responsibility for conflict with a younger child. However, age is only one way of deciding on responsibility. A normal 6-year-old may be much more responsible than a 10-year-old hyperactive child. The younger, more responsible child should be offered more incentives and rewards in exchange for greater responsibility. This will balance the scales.

When siblings fight or argue, avoid placing yourself in the middle. Do not ask who started it, what happened, or why. This will intensify rather than solve the conflict. Unless you are absolutely certain that one child is completely at fault, both children should be disciplined. This will teach them to resolve conflicts on their own and help each of them to recognize and accept an investment in their resolution.

It may also be beneficial to offer siblings what is referred to as a superordinate goal. This is an activity or reinforcement that either everyone earns or no one earns. This will help each of the siblings invest in seeing to it that everyone succeeds. Parents must be aware, however, that this also has a risk—the hyperactive sibling may still be blamed for the failure. The activity must be structured to maximize success.

Helping the Young Hyperactive Child

Because of the wide range of what is considered normal attention and activity in young children, you need to have realistic expectations of your child. If they are unrealistic, you may very quickly reinforce a pattern of problem behavior because the child cannot meet them. With younger children, it is also vital that behavior problems do not stem from other impairments such as delayed language development.

With temperamentally difficult infants and toddlers, you must understand the nature and pattern of young children's behavior, recognize the role you play in influencing it, and learn effective management skills. The manner in which you deal with your young potentially hyperactive child is a critical determinant in how much trouble the child will have in later childhood. If you approach your child with a sense of skill, patience, and tolerance, this will diffuse power struggles and prevent the development of further behavioral problems. If you approach the same child with anger, irritation, anxiety, uncertainty, and ultimately a lack of emotional closeness, this will certainly lead to a host of secondary behavioral problems.

Helping Your Hyperactive Adolescent

Most problems parents face with their hyperactive teenagers are not very different from those faced with younger hyperactive children. They often involve conflicts with rules, responsibilities, schoolwork, behavior, and sibling relationships. As noted in an earlier chapter, these problems are often intensified during normal adolescent attempts to gain some independence and separate from parents.

Today, however, very young teens perceive themselves as adult equals. This often results in an escalation of parental anger, and attempts to control. In response, hyperactive teens may become even more unpleasant, resistant, and sarcastic. Remember, hyperactive children can be more powerful than we are. This goes double for hyperactive adolescents. You are not going to resolve problems with your hyperactive teen through any of these negative means.

Author, psychologist, and teen expert Dr. Arthur Robin suggests that parents of hyperactive teens must understand eight issues. He refers to these as the "top teen survival tips of the 90's." His suggestions make sense, especially when applied in light of the other parent issues we have discussed.

1. Parents must understand normal teen development and how these factors interact with hyperactivity during the teenage years. (This was discussed in an earlier chapter.)

2. Parents must learn to offer advice, assistance, and input but not force their opinions and ideas on their hyperactive teen. A system must be established for negotiating conflicts, resolving problems and communicating effectively.

3. Parents of hyperactive teenagers must carefully choose priorities. Issues related to homework, disrespect toward authority, or sibling relationships are probably much more important than sloppy rooms or long hair.

4. Parents must use the problem-solving model described in an earlier chapter. With teens, solutions and a method to assess their success should be written down.

5. Parents must continue to manage the environment so as to minimize the hyperactive teen's problems. Remember that hyperactive teenagers do not outgrow their need for management. Without such help, your teen will not succeed.

6. Parents must establish a means of communicating effectively with their teen during times of both cooperation and conflict. Parents and hyperactive teens often regress to blaming, name calling, commanding, lecturing, and generally communicating poorly when problems cannot be solved. In the face of problems, tell your teen how you feel using an I statement rather than a you statement.

7. Continue calling on community professionals for help with communication and problem-solving skills and academic

tasks. Most hyperactive teens require some form of academic tutoring to teach organizational and planning skills, basic academic skills, or both.

8. Finally, Dr. Robin suggests that teens and parents take vacations from each other at least a few times per year for a few days at a time. This is probably a sound suggestion.

Designing the Best Home Environment for Your Hyperactive Child

Parents are frequently frustrated by the complexity of many programs for parents or for home management. Often these programs are more difficult to implement and maintain than simply tolerating the hyperactive child's behavioral difficulties would be. The following general suggestions will make life at home more bearable for your child and the entire family. The two key ideas here are consistency and organization.

Schedules. Changes in schedules and routines can be disturbing to all children but seem especially bothersome to the hyperactive child. A consistent schedule at home including specific time periods and routines for morning and evening activities, chores, homework, play time, television time, and dinner is essential. If the routine must be changed, prepare your hyperactive child ahead of time. Explain the change so that your child can anticipate what is coming.

Rules. Clear and concise rules of behavior for your hyperactive child are essential. Rules for appropriate behavior as well as consequences of breaking them should be written down and posted in a prominent place. Consistent application of the rules is essential. If a rule is broken, and it is determined that this resulted from noncompliant behavior, punishment should follow every time.

Instructions. Hyperactive children should be provided with simple, clear instructions accompanied, when possible, by demonstration. The child should then repeat them to you. A reward should be provided if the child understands and follows directions when first requested. Do not give more than one or two instructions at a time. If a task is difficult, break the task into smaller steps and then direct the child to the next step as each one is accomplished.

Controlling Stimulation. Although eliminating all distractions will not guarantee that chores and homework will be completed by your hyperactive child, such an arrangement can be beneficial. A specific, minimally distracting location should be chosen for homework completion. For younger children, play sessions should be limited to one or two children at a time. Parents may also need to take an active role in choosing appropriate playmates.

Rewards. Try to avoid setting up large, complicated reward systems consisting of toys, foods, and so on. Offer yourself and your time as a reward. Spend time with your child playing a game, visiting, talking, taking a walk, or going someplace together. When tangible rewards are used, they should be small, well-timed, and offered consistently. Remember, hyperactive children have difficulty delaying rewards. It will be difficult for your child to work throughout the week to earn one large reward at the end of the week. It may be beneficial to include a small reward for success each day and then a large reward at the end of the week if success is achieved for a consecutive number of days.

Punishment. As discussed earlier in this chapter, punishments should be brief, immediate, and consistent for noncompliant behavior. A response-cost reinforcement system should also be used.

Ignoring. Remember the power of ignoring. Ignore tolerable behavior even if you do not like it. Immediately pay attention to your child when that behavior stops and more acceptable behavior begins.

Responsibility. While it may be easier to eliminate all responsibilities from your hyperactive child, this does little to prepare the child for the realities of the world. Such an approach may also make siblings angry and antagonistic because you have set a double standard. Your hyperactive child should be provided with responsibilities that are brief and often allow the child to engage in a physical activity. If siblings have greater responsibilities, they should receive larger rewards. Complaints from brothers and sisters should be responded to with patience. Help them understand the hyperactive sibling's problems. Offer them incentives for their patience and competence.

Although participation in organized sports or other activities such as Boy Scouts may often be fraught with frustration and problems, keep trying. Find a responsive coach or understanding Scout leader. It is important for your child to be exposed to the same experiences as all other children.

Availability. You must be available to supervise your child during critical transition times such as meals, getting ready for bed, and doing homework. Anticipate situations in which problems may occur and prevent them by managing the environment. It is also essential for you to be responsible, at least through your adolescent's high school years, for seeing that he is organized, that possessions are kept in a place where they can be found, and homework is completed.

Dealing with Your Anger

Surveys have consistently demonstrated that many parents regard their parenting experiences as frustrating and negative. Parenting even normal children can be a difficult and exhausting task. Despite our best efforts, parenting requires patience, persistence, and diligence. When children do not meet our expectations, a frequent response on our part is anger. As authors Matthew McKay, Peter Rogers, and Judith McKay have noted in the book *When Anger Hurts* (New Harbinger Publications, 1989): when parents feel anxious, worry about their children, deal with stressful situations, or feel rejected, they frequently respond with anger. Anger may also be the response when children do not act the way parents wish them to or do not respond to parental pressure.

Hyperactive children very quickly can provoke anger in already frustrated parents. It is important for you to recognize this pattern and combat your angry feelings with knowledge and consistency. Remember that your anger hurts your children. Your children may perceive themselves as bad because they make you angry. Young children may be fearful and worry about being abandoned and rejected when you are angry. But most importantly, as authors McKay, Rogers and McKay note, children learn to see themselves as parents see them. If parents are insulting, threatening, or abusive, children learn to see themselves as mean, selfish, stupid, or worthless.

The most frequent misconception that triggers anger in parents of hyperactive children is the belief that their children *should* behave in certain ways. Hyperactive children frequently do not behave in ways we expect. To be an effective parent to your hyperactive child, you must recognize issues of inconsistency, incompetence, and noncompliance in your child's behavior. You must also recognize that this child, as well as all children, may not always meet your expectations. You must also recognize that high-risk situations, such as your fatigue and morning rush, may be particularly difficult and can trigger anger. You must combat anger first by recognizing it, then by restructuring your expectations, and maintaining and using a consistent set of disciplinary interventions.

Parenting Classes

The decision to participate in a parenting class should not be based solely on your child's hyperactivity, but combined with any related problems the child has. Parents of hyperactive children are often quite competent and successful in parenting their nonhyperactive children. Once they are provided with insight and education to help them understand and see the world through the eyes of their hyperactive child, they often are capable of making adjustments and

being successful parents. If your hyperactive child is also quite resistant or oppositional, a program designed to put you back in
charge should be considered. On the other hand, if your hyperactive
child is overanxious, a program designed to help you understand
your child's temperament and your effect on the child's anxiety
level would be best. A qualified professional can often be of great
assistance in helping you choose the right class.

REMEMBER . . .

✦ There are four steps to success:
  Step 1: Understand how hyperactivity affects
          your child.
  Step 2: Recognize the difference between
          noncompliance and incompetence.
  Step 3: Learn to give positive directions.
  Step 4: Build success.

✦ Your mood and temperament will affect your
  ability to deal with your child. If you are impulsive and frustrate easily, you must first learn to
  manage these problems yourself before you
  can manage your hyperactive child.

✦ Management techniques such as time out,
  positive practice, and ignoring are effective
  ways of controlling your hyperactive child's environment.

✦ Self-monitoring is an effective way of helping
  your child learn to cope with his or her inattentive, impulsive behavior.

✦ The optimal home environment for the hyperactive child should be organized; have clear
  rules, a predictable schedule, and consistent
  rewards and punishments; utilize management
  techniques and self-monitoring strategies; and
  have an available parent.

CHAPTER 11

The Need for Many Treatments

Tom is a second-grade child who has a history of inattention and hyperactivity at school. As Tom began second grade, he wanted to have a good year. However, his hyperactivity resulted in unfinished schoolwork, an inability to make friends, and alienation of the other children. The combination of schoolwork and social problems also resulted in Tom's being identified as the family problem. He began to develop a pattern of helplessness, frustration, and angry, oppositional behavior. He picked up a rock one day, out of frustration, and threw it at a car. Brief evaluation by the pediatrician resulted in a diagnosis of hyperactivity and the start of stimulant medication as the sole treatment. The medication was effective in helping Tom sit still and remain on task. He then attempted schoolwork more consistently. Unfortunately, Tom also experienced learning problems and the quality of his work did not increase significantly, but continued to be disorganized because study skills must be learned rather than swallowed. On the playground, Tom did not become frustrated quite as easily but continued to lack effective social and problem-solving skills. At home, Tom's siblings continued to identify him as the family problem, even in situations where problems did not result from his misbehavior. Medication had little impact in changing this pattern of family behavior. Finally, stimulant medication allowed Tom to plan and to act less impulsively. Instead of picking up the first rock he saw, he now looked around for a nice large one. He was also able to wait until a bus came by before throwing the rock.

PILLS WILL NOT SUBSTITUTE FOR SKILLS

The four basic skill weaknesses (inattention, impulsiveness, over-arousal, and difficulty with rewards) that characterize hyperactivity cause an extremely varied set of problems for each hyperactive child. Providing a specific treatment for a specific symptom, skill deficit, or problem may not reduce hyperactive symptoms or problems caused by other skill deficits. Problems of hyperactive children must be approached with the idea that multiple treatments are necessary if the child is going to succeed. Parents must understand and accept that hyperactivity cannot be cured. The problems of hyperactive children must be effectively managed through many different medical and nonmedical approaches.

Three kinds of intervention are used with hyperactive children. The first is medication. The second and third are nonmedical techniques that parents and teachers must understand and use. One deals with ways of effectively managing the child's home and school environment to reduce hyperactivity-related problems. A consistent morning or nighttime routine would be an example. The other consists of skill-building strategies that help the hyperactive child pay attention more effectively, plan, sit still, and control emotions. These interventions allow the child to function more effectively in the world.

MEDICATION

Medication continues to be a common and effective treatment for hyperactivity. Fifteen years ago it was suggested that at least half a million children in the United States were being treated in this way. Today, estimates are much higher.

The continued and widespread use of medications, primarily stimulants such as Ritalin in the treatment of hyperactivity, results from a demonstration by well-controlled scientific studies of a wide range of short-term positive effects. These benefits, as well as risks, will be reviewed in Chapter 12.

Over the past 10 years, the combination of the limitations of medication in solving the multiple problems of the hyperactive child, medication-related side effects and a number of promising nonmedication treatments, has led to greater interest in nonmedication therapy. The combination of the two treatments, however, is not new and has been applied over the past 20 years.

PARENT TRAINING

The second most widely used treatment for hyperactivity is parent training. These are management techniques designed to reduce problems hyperactive children experience, and skill-building techniques to increase the child's ability to deal with the world. Increasing parents' ability to understand and manage their children's problems reduces their severity, but the theoretical approaches and techniques make it difficult to draw firm conclusions about the benefits of parent training for hyperactive children. Studies have suggested, however, that there are clear, short-term positive results when parents and teachers are taught to better understand, manage, and teach their hyperactive children.

Hyperactive children are much more likely to develop negative, oppositional behavioral patterns than normal children. Mothers of hyperactive children, out of frustration, often give more directions and are more negative than mothers of normal boys. At one time, researchers thought that this parent behavior pattern resulted in child misbehavior. Now we understand, as Dr. Russell Barkley has noted, that children's behavior appears to be much more powerful in controlling parents than the other way around. In playroom settings parents' behavior improves when hyperactive children receiving medication demonstrate better attention and less noncompliance.

Based on his research, Dr. Wade Horn has suggested that problems of attention span are dealt with most effectively through the use of medication; problems with nonthinking behavior or poor planning appear to require medication and training to improve problem-solving skills. Finally, problems with academic performance may require both medication and skill building, as well as educational intervention to improve classroom functioning.

Other studies have suggested that although mothers of successfully medicated hyperactive children exhibit less negative, directing behavior, they still do not seem to exhibit as much positive behavior as the mothers of normal children. It is quite possible that in these situations, mothers of hyperactive children have simply not had the opportunity to develop alternative ways of dealing with their children. This suggests that a combination of medication (to reduce hyperactive symptoms in the child and negative responses from parents) and parent training (to improve parents' abilities to respond positively to their children and increase their children's social competence) can be most effective. However, you should not conclude from these studies that parents cannot influence the behavior of their children. They most certainly can. And it is fair to conclude that problems for the majority of hyperactive children are not caused by bad parenting.

Interventions to help hyperactive children learn more appropriate behavior have been effectively used in both home and school. The hyperactive child learns to be his own change agent.

SCHOOL

The same two sets of management and skill-building interventions are used by teachers. Interventions are modified slightly so that they are applicable to the classroom. Success in school is essential for the hyperactive child. Parents will be unable to combat 30 school hours per week of failure and frustration.

TREATMENTS SOLD FROM THE TRUNK OF THE SALESPERSON'S CAR

Although there has been some very interesting (and at times controversial) research into hyperactivity treatments (biofeedback, dietary change, megavitamin therapy, elimination of fluorescent lights, various natural substances, and attention-building through audio, visual, or computer devices) the majority of these have simply not proven to be consistently and clinically useful for a significant population of hyperactive children. Many may appear promising but more research is needed. For these reasons, we urge parents to avoid resorting to extreme treatments. While it is certainly valid to consider altering a child's diet, be wary of treatments that promise cure and offer miracles. When someone suggests that he or she can cure hyperactivity, lock the windows and run to the basement. It has also been our experience that the more extreme and fringe the treatment may be, the more expensive it usually is. Watch out for the medicine shows that come to town and, for large sums of money, offer to cure your child's problems.

WHAT DOES THIS MEAN FOR YOU?

Although it has been suggested that medication may be the most powerful treatment used for hyperactive children, medication alone is often ineffective in dealing with the variety of problems many hyperactive children experience. Additionally, parents' ability to understand the real causes of their hyperactive child's problems is also a very powerful force in determining the success of treatment. Parents able to understand that the hyperactive child's problems result from incompetence and not from purposeful noncompliance, will be more motivated, less threatened and overall less angry when they deal with their children. Hyperactive children and adolescents must also understand their disorder. Some studies have gone so far as to suggest that parent's and children's accurate knowledge of hyperactivity has an additive effect in improving behavior and in some cases, resulting in lower doses of stimulant medication use.

An effective treatment program for hyperactivity must include parents in each step of the process. Parents must also understand the need for, and goals of, various medical and nonmedical treatments for hyperactivity. Hyperactive children too must play an active role in their treatment. The Appendix contains a number of video and text resources to inform children about hyperactivity and its treatments. Remember that hyperactivity results in a number of specific skill weaknesses that can cause a variety of problems in most if not all areas of the hyperactive child's world. It is also important to remember that even the combination of treatments does not provide a cure. It has also not yet been consistently demonstrated that a combination of treatments will lead to better adult outcome than single treatments or even no treatment for hyperactive children. It is fair and accurate to state, however, that in the short term, the combination of medical and nonmedical treatments discussed in this chapter has proven extremely effective in helping hyperactive children.

REMEMBER . . .

✦ The three types of treatment used with hyperactive children are medication, management techniques, and skill-building techniques. All three of these interventions are used in the home, in the school, and on the playground.

✦ Medication continues to be a common and effective method for treating hyperactivity.

✦ The combination of all three techniques appears to hold the best promise of successfully managing hyperactive children.

✦ Problems of hyperactivity cannot be cured but must be managed.

✦ Effective management requires understanding. Parents must be involved at all steps of the evaluation and treatment process. Children must develop an understanding of their hyperactive problems.

CHAPTER 12

A Reasoned and Reasonable Approach to Using Medication with Hyperactive Children

Amy is an 8-year-old third grader. She has always had difficulty getting along with friends and sisters. Over the past three years she has had more and more difficulty completing her assignments in school. She usually forgets to bring her homework and has been unable to pass her math tests. She does not seem to be able to follow the rules when playing with other children. After a careful and thorough evaluation, it was determined that she was hyperactive. Amy began taking Ritalin and her teacher, family and friends were surprised to find that she was now able to cooperate with other students, follow the rules, and pay attention in school. She began completing her math assignments, and for the first time seemed to understand what she was supposed to be learning.

Medication, at this time, is the most effective treatment for hyperactivity, and the hyperactive child's response to medication is among the most dramatic in medicine. When some suggest that medication for hyperactivity is dangerous and others suggest that it is safe as well as effective, it is difficult to know what to think. We will try to present some of the factual basis for understanding medication. The best way to combat irrational arguments whether for or against medication is to know the facts.

Surveys of the Baltimore County schools have demonstrated the prevalence of medication in treating hyperactivity, and there has been a steady increase in the use of medication between 1971 and 1987. Current studies suggest this trend has continued. In 1987, medication was used most frequently in third graders—7% were taking it for hyperactivity. Only 1% of kindergarten and ninth-grade students were taking medication. In 1971, 40% of the medication used was Ritalin, but in 1987 it was 93%. As Ritalin is used more than other medications, we will discuss it first.

There has been much discussion of Ritalin (the brand name for the chemical methylphenidate) in the popular press. Newspaper and magazine articles, as well as television and radio talk shows present discussions of Ritalin for hyperactive behavior. People from various professions, described as experts, offer generalizations about the dangers and benefits of medication. Some suggest a high risk of drug addiction, growth suppression, psychosis, suicide, or criminal behavior, while others disagree. Exaggerated allegations make it difficult to sort out the real risk. Quotation of scientific studies often does not clarify, but rather adds more confusion to the list of side effects. Unrealistic reports and testimonials suggesting that Ritalin is a miracle without side effects adds to the confusion. A rational discussion of the genuine risks and documented benefits of Ritalin is needed to understand when medication for hyperactivity is appropriate. The decision to undertake this course of treatment should follow a careful weighing of the risks and benefits, as well as the alternatives.

RISKS OF RITALIN TREATMENT

Growth Suppression

The possibility of growth suppression has been one of the major concerns about stimulant medications. In the early 1970s, it was reported that children treated for one to three years with stimulants did not grow as fast as expected. It was later reported that children who had been taking Ritalin through the school year but had stopped it over the summer, grew faster than expected when the medication was stopped. These and similar reports prompted concern that Ritalin and other stimulants used to treat hyperactivity might suppress growth. In addition, this study suggested that periods without medication, on weekends or summer vacation for example, would help to minimize the growth suppressant effect.

Subsequent studies, however, that followed children over a longer period of time, found that after seven or eight years there was no effect on expected height or weight even when the child was taking medication every day. Study after study has suggested that growth in height and weight may be slightly suppressed over the first 6 to 18 months of treatment, but even if it is continued on a daily basis, growth is not suppressed over the long term.

Once a concern or suspicion is generated, it is difficult to get rid of it. Growth suppression with stimulant medications is one such concern. Despite many long-term studies showing no effect on height and weight, many still worry about this. Drug holidays were initially suggested as a means of avoiding this problem. But because current evidence suggests that long-term growth suppression does not occur, the underlying argument favoring drug holidays is no longer valid. Of course, children who do not experience serious problems from hyperactivity on weekends or vacations will not require medication on a seven-day basis. However, for many children symptoms continue to cause problems on weekends and vacations. When family and peer relationships are disrupted, and homework and other academic projects cannot be completed, medication may be considered appropriate for weekends and vacations.

Drug and Alcohol Addiction

Ritalin is carefully regulated by the federal government as a controlled substance, so it can only be sold with a doctor's prescription. These prescriptions are written for a maximum of one month's supply, cannot be refilled, require a new written one every month, and cannot be telephoned to the pharmacy. Substantial concern has arisen that administering controlled substances to children will promote drug or alcohol abuse and criminal behavior. Newspapers have reported crimes committed by children taking medication, and surveys of criminal populations have indicated that some criminals were given medication to treat hyperactivity symptoms in childhood. These have raised public concern that medication treatment of hyperactivity may increase the risk of drug addiction and antisocial behavior in adult life.

Unfortunately, these reports do not tell us much about the effect of Ritalin on children who take it under medical supervision. Knowing that it can be abused does not, by itself, tell us whether abuse is likely, and knowing that some criminals took medication as children does not tell us that they were criminals *because* they took medication. To determine a correlation between the effect of medication and drug abuse or criminal behavior, similar children, some treated with medication and others not so treated, must be studied over a long period of time. Studies would have had to begin with a random population of hyperactive children who were followed through adolescence to adulthood.

Long-term studies suggest that children with hyperactivity are more likely than normal children to abuse drugs and alcohol, as well as exhibit criminal behavior. Medication in childhood, however, may decrease these risks. We can conclude that treating hyperactive children with stimulant medication does not increase the likelihood of subsequent drug addiction, alcohol abuse, or criminal activity. Fear of these problems should not be a deterrent to medicating hyperactivity in childhood.

Mild Side Effects

Using the brain stem attention center model of hyperactivity discussed earlier, it is possible to understand the common side effects of stimulant medication. The positive effects result by stimulating the attention center of the brain stem. If the center that controls sleep or appetite is more sensitive to medication than the attention center, there may be a disturbance such as loss of interest in sleeping or eating. Symptoms related to stimulation of centers other than the attention center can be seen as unwanted effects, or side effects, of medication. Of children given Ritalin for hyperactivity, 20% to 50% have such unwanted effects. The three most common side effects are loss of appetite, difficulty falling asleep, and fussiness often described as irritability. It is necessary to understand that all symptoms that occur with medication are not the direct result of the medication. Some children have side effects from placebo as well.

There are several approaches to the management of these common side effects. If the symptoms are mild, they may gradually disappear with time while the medication is continued. Decreasing the dose of medication may also decrease the side effects. Allowing more time between increases of medication may result in fewer side effects for some children. Changing the hour medication is administered also will sometimes decrease side effects. If a child is not eating lunch because the medication causes loss of appetite, giving him medication after lunch may work better. Giving the first dose a little earlier in the morning may give it additional time to wear off before lunch. If sleeplessness at night is a problem, decreasing the lunchtime or afternoon dose may improve sleeping habits.

Fortunately, for most children, side effects are mild and do not last long. When the medication is continued or the amount of medication reduced, the problems usually become less severe or disappear completely. While Ritalin is by far the most popular stimulant medication (over 90% in some surveys), other similar but slightly different medications are also available. Generally, if Ritalin produces only negative effects, other stimulants will not work better. However, as discussed later in this chapter, if there are positive effects along with the side effects, alternate stimulants such as Dexedrine, Desoxyn, or Cylert may be worth a try.

For about 5% to 10% of hyperactive children, these common side effects continue to be a management problem even when the dosage or time schedule is changed. Fortunately, these common side effects resolve themselves promptly when the medication is discontinued.

Serious Side Effects

A side effect is considered to be serious if it is dramatic, prevents normal activity, and especially if it causes permanent problems. Convulsions, hallucinations, tics, and other behavior problems that do not go away after the medication is stopped, are considered serious side effects.

Some children taking Ritalin develop tics. The most common tics are eye blinking, head shaking, shoulder shrugging, or nose wrinkling. Vocal tics are also very common. A vocal tic may be as simple as a grunt, sniffle, or cough. In its worst form, children with vocal tics blurt out obscenities in a loud, uncontrolled manner that is disruptive and results in severe social consequences. These vocalizations and movements are considered tics when they are repetitive and purposeless. Children who have multiple face and body tics in addition to vocal tics, may have a disorder called Tourette's syndrome.

As many children who develop Tourette's syndrome have hyperactive behavior before other signs of Tourette's appear (approximately 50%), there is a possibility that a child who develops the disorder while taking stimulant medication may have developed Tourette's anyway, particularly if Tourette's or another movement disorder is present in the family.

Many researchers believe that stimulant medication can worsen symptoms of Tourette's syndrome and sometimes bring out symptoms before they would normally appear. These medications do not cause Tourette's syndrome. However, in most situations, children with tics should not be given stimulants and the medication should be stopped if tics develop.

There are some reasons to worry that Ritalin might actually cause Tourette's syndrome. When some children with Tourette's syndrome and hyperactivity are given Ritalin, the tics and behavior problems get worse. But some hyperactive children develop the disorder after stimulant medication is used. Not all children with

Tourette's syndrome are worse with Ritalin. While one in three of the children is worse when treated with stimulant medication, two out of three are not worsened and one in three shows a reduction in tics with stimulant medications.

About one hyperactive child in 100 develops tics when treated with stimulant medication. When the medication is discontinued, the tics almost always disappear. One study of 1,500 hyperactive children treated with Ritalin found that while 15 developed tics on medication, the tics resolved in all but one child when medication was discontinued.

Very rarely do children develop hallucinations or delusions when treated with stimulants. Only a handful of reports of children with psychotic reactions to stimulant medication are available. Studies including thousands of children taking stimulant medication do not include any who developed a psychotic reaction. In addition, when the medication is discontinued, the symptoms disappear. There are no reports of permanent psychosis or thought disorder caused by stimulant medication. While the risk of a psychotic reaction should not be ignored, we must remember that this reaction is very rare and does not appear to cause permanent problems.

BENEFITS OF MEDICATION

We believe medication for treatment of attention disorder works to improve the functioning of the brain stem attention center discussed in Chapter 3. In this way, the underlying problem causing inattention and distraction is improved. Stimulant medication, such as Ritalin, can bring about a striking change in symptoms. Seventy-five percent of hyperactive children have real improvement in their behavior. A medical treatment would be considered a success with a much lower response rate. While some children have side effects, the attention center is more sensitive than other centers in most children, and improvement in hyperactivity is often seen with few if any side effects.

Hyperactive children responding well to Ritalin demonstrate marked improvements in their attention span and a dramatic reduction in hyperactive, impulsive behavior. Their ability to remain on task, especially in boring, repetitive, or nonstimulating situations, improves to a point where they are indistinguishable from other children of their chronological age and developmental level. In situations where they must control their bodily movements and sit still for long periods of time, again their behavior is indistinguishable from others. Improvements in these areas dramatically reduce problems at home, school, and in the neighborhood. Improved attention combined with reduced restlessness at school often has a dramatic effect on increasing work completion and normalizing the hyperactive child's behavior in the classroom. Similar improvements are observed at home and on the playground. Improvements in social, family, and school functioning justify further explanation.

Social Response

When a group of normal children watch a videotape of children including a hyperactive child, they have no difficulty picking out the problem child from the other children. However, with medication the child becomes indistinguishable, and the other children cannot pick him out of the group. Improvement in behavior can be demonstrated in many others ways as well. Even the interactions between parents and their children are improved. Studies show that mothers have fewer negative interactions with their treated hyperactive children. Sometimes, the negative interactions are replaced by positive ones. At other times, there is just less mother–child contact altogether. Nonetheless, every time this issue has been studied, there was less negative interaction between the mother and her hyperactive child. Brothers and sisters likewise perceive the difference, and these relationships also improve.

But there are problems medication alone will not help. While improvement in impulsiveness, distraction, and inattention can be expected with stimulant treatment, difficulty with social skills and academic skills cannot be eliminated simply by improvement in those other areas. If under normal circumstances a child would angrily pick up a stone and throw it, his improved concentration and attention might result in looking for a larger stone and waiting to throw at a specific object. How a child responds to his new ability to concentrate and control his impulses depends on many factors. As previously noted, "Pills don't substitute for skills."

Academic Achievement

Improvement in academic achievement is not as dramatic as the improvement in behavior. Some studies of academic achievement in children who respond to stimulant medications have been disappointing. Medication treatment produces dramatic improvement in the ability to control attention and concentration. The child then pays attention, responds to the teacher, and completes and hands in the assignments. Parents and teachers are pleased and grades improve. It is natural to expect that learning will improve along with the grades. Often, the untreated hyperactive child actually understands the subject but fails due to poor behavior. As a result, failing grades quickly improve as the child hands in assignments, cooperates better with the teacher, and follows the rules. However, independent tests, which often do not show the child very far behind his peers in academic knowledge before treatment, show little improvement in academic achievement after treatment.

There have been contradictory reports about improved learning with medication. Several widely reported studies have suggested that the dosage of medication required to improve learning is different from the dosage of medication required to improve behavior. This has led some to believe that they had a choice between a medication dosage to improve learning and a medication dosage to improve behavior. Parents faced the uncomfortable situation of believing that if the medication was used to improve learning it would not improve behavior and vice versa. Fortunately, we now understand there is a direct relationship between improved behavior and improved learning. While the effects of medication on learning are not as dramatic as the effects on behavior, sensitive testing shows significant improvement in many areas of academic study. In fact, hyperactive, learning impaired children responding well to Ritalin demonstrate significantly greater academic gains than those who do not respond well.

Our brain model of hyperactivity may help explain the relationship between improved attention and learning. Academic achievement can be viewed as a function of the cerebral hemispheres, or the outer part of the brain. Attention and concentration are modulated by structures well below the cerebral cortex in the brain stem. Medication for hyperactivity improves the brain stem center for attention and concentration without directly affecting the cerebral hemispheres. Therefore, problems due to dysfunction of the cerebral hemispheres, such as learning disabilities, are not improved as dramatically as hyperactivity.

TECHNIQUES OF MEDICATION ADMINISTRATION

If Ritalin is ingested at 8:00 A.M., it reaches its maximum effectiveness two hours later at 10:00 A.M. The effectiveness then decreases over the next four hours and most of its ability to improve hyperactive behavior is gone between noon and 2:00 P.M.

Some children experience worsened behavior from six to ten hours after taking medication. This worsening of symptoms is a reaction to the withdrawal of medication rather than a direct result of the medication itself. When judging the effect of medication, it is necessary to distinguish between a direct effect and the effect of medication leaving the body. If behavior improves two hours after taking medication but worsens at six hours, teachers will see substantial improvement during school and report that the medication is working. Parents might see worsened behavior in the afternoon and evening from the rebound and conclude that the medication worsens behavior. In that example, teachers who see the medication effect and, parents who see rebound, come to opposite conclusions. A judgment about the effectiveness should take into consideration the time between medication and the observation. In a child with rebound, decreasing the morning dose is sometimes helpful.

The addition of a small second dose in the early afternoon may also help to smooth out the rebound.

Finding the Best Medication Dosage

We recommend adjusting or titrating (assessing how much of a substance is needed to produce a particular reaction) the amount of medication to fit the needs of each child rather than using a predetermined dosage schedule. Some large children do best with a low dose and some small children require a larger dose. We begin with the baseline evaluation, as discussed in previous chapters, which shows specific behavior caused by hyperactivity (target symptoms). We then prescribe with a low dose (5 mg) of Ritalin given one to two hours before the behavior usually becomes a problem. Observation of the target symptoms then shows the medication's effect. We also look for negative effects, such as worsening of some behavior and side effects on appetite and sleep as well as rebound. The whole process is then repeated for larger dosages (10, 15, or 20 mgs.). The dose that provides the greatest improvement in behavior with the fewest side effects is then continued.

As Ritalin loses its effectiveness after four hours, a multiple dose schedule is often needed. A second dose after four hours can be titrated the same way as the first dose. The optimum dose is determined by clinical reevaluation. Many children will not require a second dose and for many others the second dose is lower than the first. For these reasons separate adjustments for the morning and noon doses are recommended. Some children will require a third dose in the late afternoon and, very rarely, a fourth dose has been helpful. Most children, however, will not require more than one or two doses of medication. Judgment about medication's effectiveness must be based on observation of hyperactivity symptoms. Symptoms due to other problems such as learning disorder, anxiety, depression, or oppositional disorder are not affected by the medication. When decisions about medication are based on observation of symptoms of these other disorders, a confusing picture often develops. Positive effects on hyperactivity may be overlooked and medication appears ineffective. Other symptoms may result in inappropriate doses of medication.

Drug holidays, which may last from one day to several months, are recommended by some physicians. Initially scientific studies suggested that children who were off medication over the summer grew faster than normal. This raised a suspicion that growth was suppressed during the rest of the year. This initial suggestion has been disproven. There is no evidence that drug holidays have long-term benefits to health. Some children do not need medication outside school, but most children who benefit from medication during school also benefit on weekends and vacations. We believe that observation of behavior should determine when medication is needed.

MEDICATION FOR TEENAGERS

At one time it was commonly believed that children outgrew hyperactivity. We now understand that while symptoms of hyperactivity often change as the child becomes a teenager, they may not disappear. Some symptoms of hyperactivity persist in many, even into adulthood. Studies of school-age populations, however, show a decrease in Ritalin use in teenagers. There are most likely many reasons for this. Some teenagers do not show the same dramatic deterioration and behavior as do younger children when medication is discontinued.

It is our policy to carefully observe the child off medication once or twice a year and if no deterioration is seen, medication is not reinstituted. Other teenagers actively resist taking medication. If the family and/or child do not see a dramatic deterioration in behavior when the medication is discontinued, they may no longer follow through with it.

Another reason for decreased Ritalin use in this group is that a teenager's difficulties at school and home may involve a long history of problems with peers, family members, and teachers. The hyperactive component may be more difficult to diagnose and effectively treat with medication.

Ritalin has been shown to be an effective treatment for hyperactivity in teenagers. While other factors may make medication a less important component of the treatment program, the decision to medicate hyperactive teenagers should be based on the same principles of risk–benefit comparison that have been presented throughout this chapter. However it is essential that the adolescent understand and accept the use of medication as well as take an active role in nonmedical home and school treatments.

ADULTS

Many adults who were hyperactive as children, exhibit inattention and distractibility, as well as impulsive behavior. It is reported that some of these adults greatly benefit from stimulant medication. A word of caution, however. Children are different from adults, and scientific studies concerning the effects of medication on children do not necessarily apply to adults and vice versa. Less information is available to accurately assess either the risks or the benefits in adults.

There are other concerns about medication for adult hyperactivity. For children, the diagnosis is based on information obtained from parents, siblings, and teachers, as well as from the child. However, for adults, decisions concerning diagnosis, and effectiveness of treatment are often made from information obtained only from the patient. There is evidence that some adults with hyperactive symptoms show a substantial improvement in their behavior on stimulant medication. However, there may not be enough information about the long-term effects, both positive and negative, of stimulant medication to adequately assess and compare the risks, benefits, and alternatives of medication in adults. At this time, long-term studies of medication for hyperactive adults are underway at a number of research centers.

SUSTAINED RELEASE RITALIN

There would be many advantages of a medication that has the same positive effects as Ritalin but lasts for eight rather than four hours. Medication administered at school has several potential disadvantages whether it is given by the school or taken by the student. If the noontime dose is taken by the student, it creates a conflict with the rule of most schools requiring that school staff administer all medication. In addition, self-administered medication is often taken erratically. As it wears off, a child's inattentive, distractible, and impulsive nature often combines with the reluctance of children to take medication and may result in a missed dose. On the other hand, if the child goes to the nurse's or principal's office to receive medication, there may be a significant, negative social stigma.

When the long-acting Ritalin S.R. 20 was developed, some laboratory studies suggested it would be effective for eight hours. This would allow a single dosage of medication to last the entire school day. Early clinical trials of Ritalin S.R. 20 showed very disappointing results. Variability in onset, peak effect, and duration of activity have prevented this medication from fulfilling its promise. It is the practice of the authors to first achieve optimum results using regular Ritalin, and then substitute Ritalin S.R 20. Almost without exception, children and families have preferred the regular Ritalin. The increased effectiveness of the regular preparation more than makes up for the disadvantage of multiple dose administration. We do not begin medication therapy with Ritalin S.R. 20 because a poor response to the sustained release preparation does not necessarily mean that the child won't respond well to the regular Ritalin. Even if children seem to be responding well to the sustained release, they may respond even better to the regular Ritalin.

The latest studies have been more encouraging than the earlier ones, but the effectiveness has not yet been demonstrated in clinical use.

GENERIC METHYLPHENIDATE

Methylphenidate produced by companies other than CIBA-GEIGY is described as generic. The advantage of generic medication is the usually (but not always) lower cost. Regulations enforced by the United States government require generic medications to be equivalent to brand name medications. Equivalent does not mean identical and allows the generic tablets to contain as little as 80% or as much as 120% of the active ingredient. The variability allowed by federal guidelines may be greater than the variability regulated by the brand name manufacturer. The variability between generic and brand name medications, for example, has led the American Academy of Neurology to recommend only brand name use of certain medications in the treatment of epilepsy.

There has not been adequate study of generic methylphenidate versus Ritalin to determine whether the generic is as good for treating hyperactivity. However, it has been the experience of the authors and other clinicians that from time to time a child who responds well to Ritalin will suddenly suffer a return of symptoms when the generic drug is substituted. This child appears to no longer respond to the medication. In these unusual situations, Ritalin returns the child to effective control. As a result, it has been our practice to begin a trial of medication with Ritalin. When response is established, generic methylphenidate may be substituted. If there is an abrupt cessation of effect, the first consideration is a return to Ritalin.

OTHER STIMULANTS

Amphetamines

Amphetamine was first discovered to improve hyperactivity more than 50 years ago. One of its components, dextroamphetamine (Dexedrine), has been proven to be as effective as Ritalin by most comparative studies. Some have suggested that dextroamphetamine may have a slightly higher incidence of side effects, including suppression of height or weight and may produce more sadness in the children who take it. Overall, the effects of dextroamphetamine are very similar to that of the more popular Ritalin. Recent surveys suggest that methylphenidate is prescribed more than 10 times as frequently as dextroamphetamine for the treatment of hyperactivity. The effectiveness, duration of action, side effects, contraindications, and procedure for determining the best dose are the same for both.

The FDA has traditionally approved the use of Dexedrine for treatment of children age three or older, whereas Ritalin has been approved for children older than six. Therefore, according to these government guidelines, when medication is used for children under the age of six, Dexedrine would be the drug of choice over Ritalin. However, there are no studies that compare the two medications in children under the age of six to provide a scientific basis for the difference in the guidelines.

Methamphetamine (Desoxyn) has not been as well studied as either dextroamphetamine or methylphenidate. In principle, the action of all three should be similar.

Cylert

Pemoline (Cylert) is a stimulant that has two advantages when compared with dextroamphetamine and methylphenidate. Cylert's duration of effect is eight hours rather than the four hours for the other stimulants. Eliminating the noontime dose can be a great advantage. No additional medication is needed during school, and that avoids social stigma and missed medication. Cylert has an additional advantage. Studies have shown that animals do not develop the craving for it that they demonstrate with very high doses of Ritalin or Dexedrine. Because of this, the federal government does not place as many restrictions on the prescription of Cylert by physicians. Prescriptions for other stimulants must be in writing and cannot be telephoned in to the pharmacy, refilled, or written for more than a one-month supply. Cylert, which has fewer restrictions, can be prescribed by a telephone order to the pharmacy and one prescription can be refilled over a period of six months.

Although Cylert has some advantages, surveys suggest less than 6% of students receiving medication for treatment of attention disorders and hyperactivity receive Cylert. Several factors may account for this lack of popularity. The medication has a delayed onset of action in many children. It takes six to eight weeks before it becomes fully effective. Studies show that even after four weeks of medication therapy it had not yet significantly helped improve symptoms for some children. The other stimulants become effective the first day of therapy and reach their maximum effectiveness within two hours of administration. Delayed onset of action is one of the drawbacks of Cylert. Another drawback is that it may not be quite as effective as the other stimulants.

Concern over possible liver failure may be the most serious problem related to Cylert. In one study, blood test abnormalities suggesting liver injury in two of the children who had been taking the medication for six months, suddenly developed. While blood tests returned to normal when the Cylert was discontinued, the liver function tests became abnormal again when the medication was restarted. Neither of these children had any observed clinical symptoms (illness), and there was no sign of permanent injury. Further concern has been raised by the deaths of two children. Both are unusual circumstances. One occurred in a child described as having an overdose. The other occurred in a child with preexisting liver failure due to a birth defect (biliary atresia). In the absence of preexisting liver failure or overdose of medication, no deaths have occurred related to Cylert. As a result of these reports, blood tests to monitor liver function are suggested before Cylert is started and repeated over an extended time while it is used. The lower use of Cylert is explained by concern over the possibility of liver injury, the need for blood test monitoring, the delayed onset of action, and its lower overall effectiveness.

TRICYCLIC ANTIDEPRESSANTS

Imipramine (Tofranil) is a medication that has been widely used for treatment of several disorders, including bedwetting and depression. Because of its chemical makeup, it is in a class of medications referred to as tricyclics. Imipramine has also been widely studied as a medication for treatment of hyperactivity. It is generally effective in three out of four hyperactive children. It is usually taken in a single daily dose, avoiding the disadvantages of medication taken during school. The effectiveness of imipramine on symptoms of depression and anxiety in some children has an advantage for those hyperactive children who also have these symptoms. These advantages make imipramine a useful medication for treatment of hyperactivity.

One disadvantage is the delayed onset of action. It may take four to six weeks for imipramine to become fully effective. Another disadvantage is that it is not as effective as Ritalin. While it helps as many children as the stimulants, it has been found that imipramine does not improve hyperactivity as much as Ritalin.

Imipramine is not as easy to adjust as Ritalin. We usually recommend beginning therapy with 25 mg each evening. If no side effects are seen after an initial trial period of one week, the dose is increased to 50 mg each evening (usually at bedtime). After 50 mg has been taken for one week, a blood test (called a blood level) is done to measure the amount of the medication in the bloodstream. Improvements in the child's behavior are also evaluated at that time. While the best blood level for treatment of hyperactivity has not been determined, it is often assumed that a blood level of imipramine shown to be best for treatment of depression is also best for treatment of hyperactivity. If the amount of medication in the blood is less than 100 or more than 300, and satisfactory behavioral improvements have not been observed, the amount of medication is increased or decreased to bring the blood level within what is called the therapeutic range.

An overdose of imipramine can affect nerve impulses through the heart. In extreme cases, this can cause severe heart dysfunction and even death. The amount of imipramine required for toxic effects on the heart is generally very much higher than the amount needed for treatment of hyperactivity. A blood level determination or EKG (electrocardiogram) will show that the dosage of imipramine is not so high as to threaten heart functioning.

There are other problems seen in a few children taking imipramine. Some develop constipation and dryness of the mouth; others become sedated and quite drowsy on imipramine. Headache is a side effect seen occasionally in some children even though imipramine can be used effectively to treat headaches.

The delayed onset of action and the fact that imipramine is less effective than Ritalin for symptoms of hyperactivity probably contribute to its lack of popularity. Nevertheless, imipramine has been shown to be a safe and effective treatment for hyperactivity. Children who cannot take Ritalin because of tics, exaggerated weight loss, or other side effects, may do well on imipramine. In addition, imipramine or the chemically similar desipramine may be a good first choice for children with symptoms of both depression or anxiety and hyperactivity.

TRANQUILIZERS

The major tranquilizer, Thorazine (chlorpromazine) has been widely used for patients with very severe mental illness. In the 1960s, reports of improvement in hyperactivity suggested that Thorazine was as effective as Ritalin. However, these early studies judged improvement to be a decrease in body movement. Apparent improvement was really just sedation. While newer tranquilizers such as haloperidol (Haldol) show fewer side effects, they produce little improvement in hyperactivity. The decreased thinking ability caused by the tranquilizers is generally judged by parents, teachers, and patients as unacceptable. In addition, serious side effects such as tardive dyskinesia, characterized by writhing hands and involuntary mouth movement, are seen in some patients. These medications are not considered the front-line treatment for hyperactivity, although they are still sometimes appropriate for some children with violent or extreme behavior.

OTHER MEDICATIONS

Medications primarily used to prevent epileptic seizures, including Dilantin (diphenylhydantoin) and Tegretol (carbamazepine) have also been used to treat hyperactivity. Dilantin was believed by some in the 1960s to help hyperactivity. Careful study, however, showed that Dilantin actually worsens behavior in some children. A dramatic improvement in behavior was seen after some children who had both epilepsy and hyperactivity were changed from the sedative anticonvulsant phenobarbital to Tegretol. The change in behavior was subsequently shown to be due primarily to the elimination of the negative effects of the phenobarbital. There are several substantial disadvantages to Tegretol. Potentially fatal failure of blood-forming tissue within the bone marrow occurs in approximately one in every 200,000 patients taking the medication. In addition to the concern over this risk of death, this possibility demands that all children taking Tegretol must have frequent blood tests. While there have been reports of some children helped, the disadvantages of Tegretol take it off the list of first-line medications for treatment of hyperactivity.

Catapres (clonidine) is used to lower high blood pressure by altering metabolism of catecholamines such as noradrenaline. It also has an effect on nerve cells that utilize dopamine. Clonidine has been shown to improve hyperactivity, and it is particularly useful in children with Tourette's syndrome. In these children, it improves hyperactivity without the risk of aggravating the tics—a concern with Ritalin. Clonidine often has a sedative side effect. More studies are needed comparing the effectiveness and side effects of clonidine and Ritalin. At present it appears clonidine, while effective in selected situations, cannot be regarded as a first-line treatment for hyperactivity.

Preliminary studies of the antidepressant Prozac (fluoxetine) suggest that 50% of hyperactive children may derive benefit from this drug. It will likely not become a maintstream treatment for hyperactivity.

ALTERNATIVES TO MEDICATION

Nonmedication or behavioral interventions are an important treatment of hyperactivity. It is our recommendation that all children with hyperactivity participate in nonmedication intervention programs in addition to medication. Studies of this kind of intervention generally show it is effective at improving hyperactive behavior. There is considerable disagreement as to whether nonmedication intervention programs are more or less effective than medication intervention. Some authors have suggested that nonmedication intervention programs are equally effective. Others have suggested that nonmedication programs do not add significantly to the benefits of medication. Nonmedication intervention programs require participation of other family members, school personnel, and more assistance from professional counselors. As a result, these programs are more costly, both in terms of time and expense. Some benefits from nonmedication intervention cannot be achieved with medication. For example, social skills training, specific educational supplementation, psychotherapy, and environmental management programs can provide help for the hyperactive child.

Long-term studies have usually demonstrated surprisingly little long-term effect either with medication or behavioral interventions. While some studies have suggested that a combination of medication and nonmedication interventions undertaken for three years or longer will have long-term positive effects, the majority of studies fail to show significant long-term benefits of medication intervention. When stimulant medication is considered, keep in mind that there may well be no discernible effect on the adult outcome as the result of either medication or nonmedication intervention programs. This information does not diminish the value of the immediate gain to the child in both academic and social improvement. Children treated with stimulant medication for hyperactivity in childhood recall their childhood with more positive memories than children who were not treated.

Comparison of the risks and benefits with the alternatives to stimulant medication provides a sound background for determining the appropriateness of medication intervention.

REMEMBER . . .

✦ The decision to undertake medication intervention should be made only after careful consideration of both the risks and benefits of medication.

✦ Medication can be a highly effective treatment and improve the ability of the child to control the symptoms of hyperactivity.

✦ Ritalin is by far the most widely used medication to treat attention disorders.

✦ Ritalin's risks include mild side effects such as loss of sleep or appetite, as well as rare, severe side effects, including psychosis or convulsions. These problems do not result in permanent injury.

✦ If children develop tics on Ritalin, in most situations the medication should be discontinued.

✦ Tourette's syndrome can be aggravated by Ritalin, but current thinking suggests Ritalin does not cause Tourette's syndrome.

✦ Dexedrine is as effective as Ritalin but may cause slightly more side effects.

✦ Cylert works almost as well as Ritalin but fear of liver injury and the need for blood tests limit its use.

✦ Imipramine and desipramine may be good alternatives to Ritalin.

✦ While many other medications have been tested, none are as effective and safe as the stimulants (Ritalin, Dexedrine, Desoxyn, and Cylert) or the tricyclics (Tofranil).

PART IV

AFTERWORD

CHAPTER 13

Final Thoughts on Hyperactivity

Someday the mysteries of heredity and brain function may be discovered. When that time arrives, we may gain an important understanding of many human behaviors, including hyperactivity. Ultimately with understanding may come a cure. Until that time, parents and professionals must work hand in hand responsibly to define, observe, evaluate, and manage hyperactivity in childhood.

The common-sense definition of hyperactivity must serve as a guideline to help you understand your child's inability to meet the demands of the world we have constructed. For now hyperactivity is a problem that must be managed and cannot be cured. Effective management requires understanding. It is essential that parents and their hyperactive children develop a common-sense understanding of hyperactive problems. Because the multiple behavioral problems of hyperactive children may be easily mislabeled and misunderstood, parents must understand the issue of incompetence versus noncompliance in dealing with these problems.

Hyperactivity is a disorder that must also be understood from a developmental perspective. Problems with attention span, emotionality, restlessness, impulsiveness, and difficulty delaying rewards will have a very different impact on children of different ages. Although a group of hyperactive children may share many similar skill deficiencies, any two children compared randomly within the group may be experiencing very different problems. Remember, being hyperactive does not predict that your child will experience a certain set of problems. Remember also that this is a disorder of consistency and not necessarily ability.

Because symptoms of hyperactivity can be exhibited by children experiencing other childhood problems, careful evaluation is essential. Medical, educational, psychological, and behavioral information must be gathered, organized, and evaluated. Evaluation of your child's hyperactivity is incomplete if it does not help you and your child's teachers understand the powerful impact hyperactivity may be having on the child.

The current multitreatment philosophy for hyperactivity requires that each child's problems be addressed in a comprehensive fashion. A single treatment approach has not and will not prove effective in dealing with all the problems hyperactive children experience. Education, behavior management, group and individual counseling, educational intervention, and medication have proven to be an appropriate set of treatments for hyperactivity. Effective evaluation and management of hyperactivity is a reality, but it requires time, effort, caring, and understanding.

Some of the statistics and information presented in this book are certainly of concern and may be worrisome for parents. There appears to be a significant group of hyperactive children who may grow into, as opposed to out of, their hyperactivity. There appears to be a group who experience problems with conduct. The occurrence of hyperactivity and conduct difficulty appears to dramatically increase the chances that a teenager or adult may experience problems academically, at work, with family, and with the rules of society. It is important, however, to remember that this information is based on studies of large groups of people. The potential outcome for any one individual is determined by many forces. Thus, these group data may not be very helpful when trying to understand your hyperactive child. We must not ignore this information. It helps us understand that hyperactive children risk problems in later life. We must also not assume a catastrophe based on this information either. It might be best, therefore, to leave you with the story of John, a young man we have had the opportunity to evaluate and work with over the past five years. His history and success teach us a very important lesson about hyperactive children.

John was the second in his family of six children. John's mother recalled that as an infant he was extremely irritable, restless, and did not fit into routines well. He was constantly into things as a toddler and very quickly stretched his parents' patience. He had very little difficulty learning, but his teachers reported that he rarely paid attention and often left his work uncompleted. By fourth grade, John was referred for evaluation because of his school and home problems. He was found to be very intelligent and did not have a learning disability. He was, however, diagnosed as hyperactive. By junior high school the increasing demands of school overwhelmed even John's superior intelligence. John's parents also recalled that he was isolated socially and could never seem to learn to deal appropriately with his friends.

At home, John would manipulate or intimidate other family members to get his way. He terrorized his siblings. His sister recalled locking herself in her bedroom when her parents were not home and John lost his temper. Although John's problems with inattention and hyperactivity improved as he grew older, he continued to have a short temper. He would frustrate easily and at times act in an unreasonable fashion. He was a significant discipline problem for his parents.

Over the years, John's family sought help from a number of professionals. In addition to the diagnosis of hyperactivity, they were provided with a number of other diagnoses. Various medical and nonmedical treatments were recommended. Nothing seemed to help very much.

We evaluated John as he began his senior year in high school. The symptoms of hyperactivity were still quite prevalent. Nonetheless, John was slowly maturing. He was gaining in his ability to relate socially. He had also learned how to succeed in high school. Our assessment continued to reflect John's superior intelligence while indicating that he still had problems with attention span, planning, and organization. John was aware of his impulsiveness, inattention, and hyperactivity. His personality was shaped by years of hyperactivity and frustration. He was overly self-critical and had difficulty solving problems and compromising with others.

As John was doing well in school, a course of nonmedical intervention was initiated. Through weekly counseling, John's understanding of himself and his personality increased. His interpersonal skills improved. Though he made slow but steady progress at home, at school, and with friends, it was painful at times as John wrestled with years of frustration.

John graduated from high school successfully, and he recently completed a two-year mission for his church. Although he struggled initially on his mission, he eventually gained confidence and learned to relate well with his mission partners.

When John returned from his mission, he called the authors to set up a visit to help him plan to enter college. Over the telephone, John reported that he had learned to master his attention problems and was more organized. He made a point of noting that he was writing down the appointment time in his day planner. Unfortunately, John neglected to check the planner and missed his appointment. A day later John called to apologize and reschedule. He spontaneously commented that he was still struggling with his hyperactivity. Even his attempts at managing problems were not always successful. Nonetheless, John appeared happy, aware of his hyperactivity, and frequently able to use strategies to compensate. At the time of this writing, struggling with the demands of college, John requested a referral to an adult psychiatrist to consider medication.

Although it seems contradictory, John is and will continue to be a successful, hyperactive, young adult. We are confident that John will make a positive contribution to our society.

A CHECKLIST FOR SUCCESS

We leave you with the following checklist for success. The combination of all these elements, consistently and patiently applied as your child grows, will lead to a happy, successful, achieving, although still hyperactive, child.

_____ *Educate Yourselves.* The more you understand your child and yourself, the more success you will have. Knowledge is your most effective intervention with your hyperactive child.

_____ *Effective Management Strategies at Home.* You must develop one set of interventions to deal with problems of incompetence and another set to deal with problems of noncompliance.

_____ *Parental Unity.* You and other adults who interact with your child on a regular basis must use a consistent set of interventions, applied fairly and routinely.

_____ *Positive Parent–Child Relationships.* Seek out that which you both enjoy and, on a daily basis, participate in those activities.

_____ *Family Stability.* Your hyperactive child may be a barometer for family problems. Deal with problems as they occur. Try to avoid crises.

_____ *Good Friends.* Social success is an essential component for dealing with hyperactivity.

_____ *Problem-Solving Training.* Teach your child a model for solving problems that can be used consistently.

_____ *School Success.* Be patient, persistent, and proud.

_____ *Do Not Ignore Nonhyperactive Problems.* Your hyperactive child risks developing other behavioral or learning problems. They must be addressed as well.

_____ *Medical Treatment.* Many hyperactive children may not require medication, but when the benefits outweigh the risks, medication can be an important and useful part of the treatment plan.

Appendix

RESOURCES FOR PARENTS

Pamphlets

A Parent's Guide: Attention-Deficit Hyperactivity Disorder in Children (1989, 2nd edition) by Sam Goldstein, PhD, and Michael Goldstein, MD. Available from The Neurology, Learning and Behavior Center, 230 South 500 East, Suite 100, Salt Lake City, Utah 84102.

Attention Deficit Hyperactivity Disorder and Learning Disability: A Booklet for Parents (1989) by Larry B. Silver, MD. Available from CIBA Pharmaceuticals, 556 Mars Avenue, Summit, New Jersey 07901, Attention: Marketing Services.

ADHD Hyperactive Children by A. Mervyn Fox, MD. Available from Gordon Systems, Inc., P.O. Box 746, DeWitt, New York 13214.

Books

Clark, L. (1986). *SOS: Help for Parents.* Bowling Green, Kentucky: Parents Press.

Fowler, M. (1990). *Maybe You Know My Kid: A Parent's Guide to Identifying, Understanding and Helping Your Child with ADHD.* New York: Birchlane Press.

200 ✦ Afterword

Friedman, R.J., and Doyal, G.T. (1987). *Attention Deficit Disorder and Hyperactivity* (2nd ed.). Danville, Illinois: Interstate Printers and Publishers, Inc.

Gordon, M. (1990). *ADHD/Hyperactivity: A Consumer's Guide.* DeWitt, New York: GSI Publications.

Ingersol, B. (1988). *Your Hyperactive Child: A Parent's Guide to Coping with Attention Deficit Disorder.* New York: Doubleday Books.

Parker, H. (1988). *The Hyperactivity Workbook for Parents, Teachers and Kids.* Plantation, Florida: Impact Publications.

Phelan, T. (1985). *1-2-3 Magic: Training Your Preschoolers and Preteens to Do What You Want.* Glen Ellyn, Illinois: Child Management Press.

Phelan, T. (1990). *Hyperactivity and Attention Deficit Disorders.* Glen Ellyn, Illinois: Child Management Press.

Taylor, J.F. (1990). *Helping Your Hyperactive Child.* Rocklin, California: Prima Publishing.

Turecki, S., and Tonner, L. (1985). *The Difficult Child.* New York: Bantam Books.

Wender, P.H. (1987). *The Hyperactive Child, Adolescent, and Adult: Attention Deficit Disorder through the Life Span.* New York: Oxford University Press.

Textbooks

Barkley, R.A. (1990). *Attention-Deficit Hyperactivity Disorder: A Handbook for Diagnosis and Treatment.* New York: Guilford Press.

Goldstein, S., and Goldstein, M. (1990). *Managing Attention Disorders in Children: A Guide for Practitioners.* New York: John Wiley & Sons.

Videotapes

Barkley, R.A. (1990). *AD/HD Video*. Available from NEAD, P.O. Box 82, Northboro, Massachusetts 01532-0082.

Copeland, E.D. (1989). *Understanding Attention Disorders: Preschool through Adulthood*. Atlanta, Georgia: 3 C's of Childhood, Inc.

Garfinkel, B.D. (1991). *Creative Approaches to Attention Deficit Hyperactivity Disorder (ADHD): Active Partnerships*. Available from the University of Minnesota, Department of Professional Development.

Goldstein, S. (1989). *Why Won't My Child Pay Attention?* Available from The Neurology, Learning and Behavior Center, 230 South 500 East, Suite 100, Salt Lake City, Utah 84102. This video has won five awards, including the New York Film Festival.

Audio Cassettes

Parker, H. (1990). *Listen, Look and Think: A Self-Regulation Program for Children*. Impact Publications, 300 N.W. 70th Avenue, Suite 102, Plantation, Florida 33317.

INFORMATION AND SUPPORT GROUPS FOR PARENTS

ADDA (Attention Deficit Disorder Association)
(Association of Local Support Groups for ADD)
4300 West Park Blvd.
Plano, Texas 75093

This nationally represented group is a consortium of local support groups for families of children with attention disorder. They are an excellent referral source and well aware of the majority of support groups throughout the country.

ADDAG (Attention Deficit Disorder Advocacy Group)
8091 South Ireland Way
Aurora, Colorado 80016
(303) 690-7548

This parent organization is very active in providing support to parents, professionals and educators. They publish a very informative monthly newsletter.

ATTENTION Please!
Bi-monthly Newsletter for Children with ADD
2106 3rd Avenue North
Seattle, Washington 98109-2304

CH.A.D.D. (Children with Attention Deficit Disorder)
Parent Support Group - Chapters Nationwide
499 N.W. 70th Ave., #308
Plantation, Florida 33317
(305) 587-3700

This organization is comprised of almost 300 chapters nationally and internationally. They are dedicated to providing support and information to parents and professionals. They are an excellent source to help parents identify local resources.

Self-Help Clearing Houses
(For Assistance in Finding Informing Self-Help Groups)

Self-Help Clearing House, New Jersey
(201) 625-7101
Self-Help Center, Illinois
(312) 328-0470
National Self-Help Clearing House, New York
(212) 840-1259

The Coordinating Council for Handicapped Children
20 East Jackson Blvd., Room 900
Chicago, Illinois 60604
(312) 939-3513

This advocacy group publishes several manuals and brochures concerning parent advocacy and services available for handicapped children.

Counseling Care Services
300 Northwest 70th Avenue, #102
Plantation, Florida 33317
(305) 792-8100

Information Center for Handicapped Children
605 "G" Street, N.W., 2nd floor
Washington, DC 20001

Learning Disability Association
(Local chapters throughout the country)
National Headquarters
4156 Library Road
Pittsburgh, Pennsylvania 15234
(412) 341-1515

> The LDA is a nonprofit, national organization concerned with the education of children with learning disabilities and attention disorders. It publishes a newsletter five times per year and has local and state chapters throughout the country.

Learning Disabilities Associations of Canada
Alberta
145-11343-61st Avenue
Edmonton T6H 1M3
(403) 448-0360

British Columbia
203-15463-104th Avenue
Surrey V3R 1N9
(604) 588-6322

Manitoba
301-960 Portage Avenue
Winnipeg R3G 0R4
(204) 774-1821

Saskatchewan
Albert Community Centre
26-610 Clarence Avenue S.
Saskatoon S7H 2E2
(306) 652-4114

Ontario
124 Merton St., 3rd Floor
Toronto M4S 2Z2
(416) 487-4106

Quebec (Aqeta)
300-284 rue Notre-Dame O
Montreal H2Y 1T7
(514) 847-1324

New Brunswick
138 Neil Street
Fredericton E3A 2Z6

Nova Scotia
55 Ochterloney Street
Dartmouth B2Y 1C3
(902) 464-9751

Prince Edward Island
P.O. Box 1081
Charlottetown C1A 7M4
(902) 892-9664

Newfoundland
P.O. Box 8632, Station A
St. John's A1B 3T1
(709) 754-3665

Northwest Territories
P.O. Box 242
Yellowknife X1A 2N2
(403) 873-6378

Yukon Territory
P.O. Box 4853
Whitehorse Y1A 4N6
(403) 668-5167

Learning Development Services
3754 Clairemont Drive
San Diego, California 92117
(619) 276-6912

The Mercury Center
3300 S. Main Street
Anderson, Indiana 46013
(317) 640-2343

The National Center for Children with
Learning Disabilities
99 Park Avenue
New York, New York 10016

The NCLD is a fund-raising organization sponsoring research and advocacy programs for children with learning disabilities. They publish a magazine yearly.

The Neurology, Learning and Behavior Center
230 South 500 East, Suite 100
Salt Lake City, Utah 84102
(801) 532-1484

PACER Center
(Parents Advocacy Coalition for Educational Rights)
4826 Chicago Avenue South
Minneapolis, Minnesota 55417-1055
(612) 827-2966

The Parent Educational Advocacy Training Center
228 South Pitt Street, Suite 300
Alexandria, Virginia 22314

Parents' Place
103, 1010 - 4 Avenue South
Lethbridge, Alberta T1J 0P5

Tourette's Syndrome Association
National Headquarters
42-40 Bell Blvd.
Bayside, New York 11361
(718) 224-2999

RESOURCES FOR CHILDREN AND ADOLESCENTS

Goldstein, S. (1991). *It's Just Attention Disorder: A Video Guide for Kids.* This video has won three major awards. Salt Lake City, Utah: Neurology, Learning and Behavior Center.

Gordon, M. (1991). *Jumpin' Johnny. Get Back to Work: A Child's Guide to ADHD/Hyperactivity.* DeWitt, New York: GSI Publications.

Gordon, M. (1992). *My Brother's a World Class Pain: A Sibling's Guide to ADHD/Hyperactivity.* DeWitt, New York: GSI Publications.

Moss, D.M. (1989). *Shelly the Hyperactive Turtle.* Kensington, Maryland: Woodbine House Publishers.

Nadeau, K. and Dixon, E. (1991). *Learning to Slow Down and Pay Attention.* Plantation, Florida: Impact Publications.

Parker, R.N. (1992). *Making the Grade: An Adolescent's Struggle with ADD.* Plantation, Florida: Impact Publications.

Quinn, P.O., and Stern, J.M. (1991). *Putting on the Brakes: Young People's Guide to Understanding Attention Deficit Hyperactivity Disorder.* New York, New York: Imagination Press.

RESOURCES FOR EDUCATORS

Pamphlets

A Teacher's Guide: Attention-Deficit Hyperactivity Disorder in Children (1991, 2nd edition) by Sam Goldstein, PhD., and Michael Goldstein, MD. Available from The Neurology, Learning and Behavior Center, 230 South 500 East, Suite 100, Salt Lake City, Utah 84102.

Attention Deficit Hyperactivity Disorder: A Booklet for the Classroom Teacher (1990) by Larry B. Silver, MD. Available from CIBA Pharmaceuticals, 556 Mars Avenue, Summit, New Jersey 07901 (Attention: Marketing Services).

Books

Barkley, R.A. (1990). *Attention-Deficit Hyperactivity Disorder: A Handbook for Diagnosis and Treatment.* New York: Guilford Press.

Braswell, L., Bloomquist, M., and Pederson, S. (1991). *A Guide to Understanding and Helping Children with ADHD in School Settings.* Minneapolis, Minnesota: University of Minnesota.

Copeland, E.D., and Love, V.L. (1990). *Attention without Tension: A Teacher's Handbook on Attention Disorders (ADHD and ADD).* Atlanta, Georgia: 3 C's of Childhood, Inc.

Goldstein, S., and Goldstein, M. (1990). *Managing Attention Disorders in Children: A Guide for Practitioners.* New York: John Wiley & Sons, Inc.

Jones, C. (1991). *Sourcebook for Children with Attention Deficit Disorder in Early Childhood.* Tucson, Arizona: Communication Skill Builders.

Kirby, E.A., and Grimley, L.K. (1986). *Understanding and Treating Attention Deficit Disorder.* New York: Pergamon Press.

McCarney, S.B. (1989). *The Attention Deficit Disorders Intervention Manual.* Columbia, Missouri: Hawthorne Educational Services.

Parker, H. (1992). *The ADD-Hyperactivity Handbook for Schools.* Plantation, Florida: Impact Publications.

Videotapes

Copeland, E.D. (1990). *ADHD/ADD Video Resource for Schools.* Atlanta, Georgia: 3 C's of Childhood, Inc.

Goldstein, S., and Goldstein, M. (1990). *Educating Inattentive Children.* Available from The Neurology, Learning and Behavior Center, 230 South 500 East, Suite 100, Salt Lake City, Utah 84102. This video has won three awards.

Index